A SHORT GUIDE TO

SPIRITUAL DISCIPLINES

A SHORT GUIDE TO

SPIRITUAL DISCIPLINES

How to Become a Healthy Christian

MASON KING

B&H
PUBLISHING
BRENTWOOD, TENNESSEE

978-1-0877-6848-9

Published by B&H Publishing Group
Brentwood, Tennessee

Dewey Decimal Classification: 248.84
Subject Heading: CHRISTIAN LIFE \
SPIRITUAL LIFE \ DISCIPLESHIP

Cover design and illustration by Matt Lehman.
Author photo by Lindsey Brittain.

1 2 3 4 5 6 • 26 25 24 23

Dedication

Piper, Sheppard, and Posey

In life there will be plenty of distractions from God's good design. Root your loves in Christ, God's best given for you. This is the great work of your life, that you might become who He has made you to be and image His goodness to the world. Make your home next to the river of God's love.

I'm proud of you, and I will always love you
more than you know.

Dad

Birdie,

I love you. I am more grateful every year for the life we have together. I have learned to love being loved by you.

MK

How much are you willing to invest in yourself? People think they can look like giant oaks without putting down deep roots. When they realize how much effort it takes to put down deep roots, they settle for being bramble bushes. To be who you really are takes work, but it is good and rewarding work. "To be a human," Augustine argues, "is to be the consistent, enduring subject of one's deliberations and actions." Anyone can rebel, and anyone can acquiesce, but it takes real effort to be a person. People often complain that they are not who they should be, but they take no action to change.

—KLYNE R. SNODGRASS, *WHO GOD SAYS YOU ARE*

Contents

Foreword

I HAVE ENJOYED THE privilege of ministry partnership with my friend Mason King for the better part of ten years. I want to tell you a little of what friendship with Mason looks like. It looks like the spontaneous gift of an antique set of books by one of your favorite authors. It looks like your favorite dessert appearing at the end of a dinner in his home. It looks like an action figure of one of your heroes left as a surprise on your desk. It's a line of George Herbert poetry he knows will make you cry, or a paragraph from a commentary he knows will harmonize with what you're studying. You don't really remember when you told him you liked Dickens or cinnamon ice cream or poetry, or that you were studying atonement theory, but he remembers anyway. Because when he's with you, you have the best gift of all: his full attention.

I think being with Mason probably feels a lot like being with Jesus. Full focus, full investment. The feeling of being seen and known and valued. In an age of distractions and diversions,

Mason King has chosen and followed quiet habits that anchor him in service to God and others. He has chosen patterns that free him to consider others more highly than himself. He has chosen the way of Jesus.

As I read the words of this book, I re-lived conversations we have shared about simplicity and self-awareness, about Sabbath, and long horizons of faithfulness, about the place of our feelings in relation to our faith, and about the shared burdens and joys of Christian community. I remembered sermons I have heard him preach that cut me to the heart with their gentle calls to holiness. And I remembered not merely his words, but the ways I have witnessed first-hand the fruit of these meditations in the life of a man who lives what he believes—fruit evident in his family, in his friendships, and in his church.

If you were friends with my friend, I can promise you he would anticipate what would bring you joy just as he has done for me and so many others. But even if you never know him personally, that is exactly what he is giving you in the pages of this book. A life patterned on the way of Jesus is a life of joyful discipline. What a gift to be reminded, "This is the way, walk in it."

Jen Wilkin, author and Bible teacher

Author's Note

EVERY NONFICTION BOOK GETS written because someone has a view they want to convince you is true. Here's mine, up front:

The triune God of the Bible is who He says He is, and what He says about you is true. Our culture tells us that truth is fluid, sin is fiction, and to hold a belief that contradicts someone else's feelings, experience, or interpretation of their life is unloving, intolerant, or small-minded.

We are rapidly reducing the beauty of being made in God's image to our own definition of comfort, pleasure, and self-fulfillment—which repeatedly fail to bring about the life offered by God.

You may wrestle with what level of change to expect in life. Looking at our own choices and those of Christians around us, I can understand. We live with overpromised or under-hoped-for expectations for the kind of change we can experience as Christians. At the same time, the world offers a compelling invitation to fulfill our desires outside of God's good design. It's easy to choose comfort over character, especially if we're confused about who God is and who we're supposed to become.

> The question we often ask is: "What am I supposed to do?"
>
> The question we need to ask is: "What kind of person do I need to become?"

Spoiler alert: God isn't hiding the answer. Our culture has opted out of God's view of reality, so it takes work for us to see and live in His story. We value proven facts, predictable results, and short-term gains without long-term effort. We want decades of life change in weeks, and when quick results don't come, we move on to the next thing.

In our backyard there is an oak tree, full of years and character. Most mornings before the sun rises, before I begin my morning disciplines, I sit and study the tree out the living room window. I treasure these quiet moments, becoming present to God in a new day.

In the end I want my life to be as steady, strong, and noble as that tree. I want to offer an oak of righteousness to Jesus, a life daily nourished by God's living water as He works in me a heart surrendered to Him.

Friend, I want that for you. Oaks don't grow overnight; they take decades to mature. You and I have been invited to plant our lives next to the river of God's love. This is our daily work, living with the end in mind.

My prayer is that our conversation will serve in this, the great work of your life. May you hear and respond to the call of becoming who God made you to be over a lifetime for His glory, your good, and the good of those around you.

Mason King

Introduction

NO ONE PICKS UP a book on spiritual disciplines without an eye toward the future—the future Christian life they want to live, the future maturity level they might attain, the future version of themselves they want to be. If you've come to this book, it's probably because you are thinking about your spiritual future. You want to change. You want to grow. You want to become a healthier Christian, and so do I! Before we get started, let me remind you of something my pastor regularly reminds our church: God is not waiting for a future version of you to love.

If you are a Christian, it can be easy to assume familiarity with Jesus. Who He is, what He has done, what He is doing and will do—check. When we do this, however, life with God quickly becomes stop this, do that, then you'll be lovable.

We begin with faith, expect change, and are painfully aware of failure. We think trying harder will take care of the shame we feel for the things we just can't quit. Frustrated with ourselves, we figure if God is real, He's probably frustrated with us too. This is when we doubt God could love like we've been told.

Here's the thing: God is real, He can be trusted, and He loves *you*.

God doesn't tolerate you. God *loves* you. God loves *you*.

I struggled with this for years. I knew I was in God's family, but I hung out by the front door of the house. I was nervous that at some point I'd be found out and need to make a quick exit. It felt like God loved other people, but I was unworthy, too complicated, or was close to using up all my chances.

Jesus told his disciples: "As the Father has loved me, I have also loved you" (John 15:9).

Me? I know me. You must mean someone else. I can often focus on being a fallen sinner at the expense of believing I'm a beloved son. I know where I fail. I don't need a reminder.

How about you?

Are you willing to take God at His Word? Christ loves you, and it's not despite who you are. How you've made your way in the world so far won't keep you from Him. He *already* loves you and invites you to live life as He designed it to be.

God is not waiting for a future version of you to love ***and*** **He has a future version of you in mind.**

This future you is *you*, with all your gifts and character—renewed and transformed in the image of your Maker. It's not as if your gifts, character, and experience don't matter. Christ takes all of you and offers the opportunity to become fully human, as you and I are made to be. This is what spiritual disciplines are all about, really.

God works to restore in us the ability to delight in the true, the beautiful, and the good. He calls us to join Him in forming our character because we live in a world that is actively trying to *de*form us into its own image. We are invited to life with Him, full of purpose and meaning, laughter and deep joy.

As you consider what living a fully formed life in Christ might look like as you pursue spiritual disciplines, spend some time praying and answering the following questions. Write them down so you can refer back to them.

1. Who do you hope to become?

What adjectives do you want others to use when they describe you in five years? (for example, disciplined, kind, generous)

2. Who are you becoming today?

If who you are today is the product of the choices from all your yesterdays, who are you becoming right now? How would others describe you today if they watched your life over the last year?

3. How do you think God describes you *right now*?

What do you tell yourself God thinks about you?

When you look at the whole of your answers to question 3, are they representative of the God of the Bible? Often this list shows us more about our sources of shame than our salvation.

What do you notice about your answers to questions 1 and 2? Are there any themes or patterns?

In being faced with the gap between who we want to be and who we're becoming, your response is important. One author helps us think about it like this:

> There is no way forward unless we are willing to be displeasing to ourselves. . . . In other words, we will not change unless we are dissatisfied with who we are. If we are not willing to examine ourselves, be honest, and admit our shortcomings even when it hurts, we will never be who God calls us to be.[1]

How do I become who God has made me to be? How do I ensure that tomorrow's "me" is spiritually healthier than today's? That's the question we're setting out to answer in the pages that follow. And though the answer is not easy, it is simple: you become a healthier, truer, and more Christian you by not only understanding what a healthy life with God is but by disciplining yourself in three crucial areas in order to get there.

As you read, know that this book may feel different to you than typical spiritual discipline books that are filled with to-do lists. Practical ideas for spiritual development are indeed found within these pages, yes, but this book is not merely going to tell you to read your Bible and pray. It will *include* those disciplines, yes, but it is going to offer you much more. It's going to give you a fuller picture of what it means to have healthy spiritual habits—a picture of what life looks like when you discipline yourself to offer *all* of your life to God instead of just the minutes dedicated to prayer, evangelism, church attendance, Bible reading, and so on.

This work consists of two sections, and we'll cover the following in them:

SECTION I: A HEALTHY LIFE WITH GOD

- What informs and influences how we think about God, ourselves, and our lives.
- Build perspective about who we're actually becoming and how God may be working to mind the gap between this and who God made us to be.

SECTION II: THREE DIMENSIONS FOR A HEALTHY LIFE WITH GOD

The remainder of the book is an invitation to practice being present with God in three areas of daily life. The categories are purposefully broad, and in each we explore a set of disciplines to help you sow toward your future self. These practices aid us in becoming the kind of person that, over time (and through grace), increasingly displays the fruit of the Spirit. These three dimensions are:

- Our ***attention***, the most precious commodity we have. Who you are today is built on where your attention went yesterday. If you want a future self that is healthier in Christ than you are today, then disciplining your attention is nonnegotiable.
- Our ***emotions***. God created emotions, and Jesus experienced and stewarded every emotion perfectly in the flesh. He showed us how to manage, and not be managed by, emotions. If you discipline yourself to give your emotional life to God on a regular basis as Jesus did, the you of tomorrow will be more like Christ.

- Our ***limits***. We have a Creator, and we are not that Creator, yet often we view our limits as obstacles instead of as mercies. The life of self-sufficiency is a repeated declaration of independence from God, and this is not the call of the Christian. If you want to get healthier as a Christian, you'll need to get disciplined in the way you embrace the boundaries of your creaturehood.[2]

As I said before, these three categories—***attention***, ***emotions***, and ***limits***—are purposefully broad. The suggested disciplines within each are starting points for training in godliness, not checklists to accomplish. These disciplines orient us first to God, then to ourselves, and finally outward to others. The order is important here. Plenty of best-selling advice for the good life misses the first and third steps, directing you toward yourself—and yourself *only*—as the origin and object of change.

God knows what we need, and He has provided for us in Jesus. Through the Bible, God invites you to an eternal quality of life, the life you are designed to live. He invites you to know, love, trust, and obey Jesus, to be renewed in the image of your Maker. No hidden agenda, no scam, no other shoe waiting to drop. You can trust God, both for now and for who He has called you to become.

When faced with who they want to be and who they are actually becoming, many Christians feel shame thinking they should be further along by now.

These shame-filled accusations can take different, but similar, forms:

> *"Look at them. They're near your age but are so much more godly than you—what happened?"*
>
> *"You're not lovable. Just look at the choices you've made. Grace is for other people."*
>
> *"You're twenty years into life with Christ and still struggling with the same cycles of sin. God has to be disappointed with the mess you've made of your life."*

When I hear these accusations, the parable of the workers in the vineyard is an encouragement to my heart. Jesus has been teaching about how the first will be last, and then disciples start arguing about who will be the greatest among them. A few even get their mom involved to ask Jesus for special treatment, and He responds:

> "For the kingdom of heaven is like a landowner who went out early in the morning to hire workers for his vineyard. After agreeing with the workers on one denarius, he sent them

into his vineyard for the day. When he went out about nine in the morning, he saw others standing in the marketplace doing nothing. He said to them, 'You also go into my vineyard, and I'll give you whatever is right.' So off they went. About noon and about three, he went out again and did the same thing. Then about five he went and found others standing around and said to them, 'Why have you been standing here all day doing nothing?'

"'Because no one hired us,' they said to him.

"'You also go into my vineyard,' he told them. When evening came, the owner of the vineyard told his foreman, 'Call the workers and give them their pay, starting with the last and ending with the first.'

"When those who were hired about five came, they each received one denarius. So when the first ones came, they assumed they would get more, but they also received a denarius each. When they received it, they began to complain to the landowner: 'These last men put in one hour, and you made them equal to us who bore the burden of the day's work and the burning heat.'

> "He replied to one of them, 'Friend, I'm doing you no wrong. Didn't you agree with me on a denarius? Take what's yours and go. I want to give this last man the same as I gave you. Don't I have the right to do what I want with what is mine? Are you jealous because I'm generous?'
>
> "So the last will be first, and the first last." (Matt. 20:1–16)

We compare ourselves to others; we create standards of perfection Superman couldn't reach, and we believe we're no good when we fail.

Jesus sets the standard of relationship at His generosity, not your maturity.

We are all an ongoing process of change until the day we die.[3] In the end, the beauty we're wanting, the lightness and joy we long for are found not in an idea or a habit but in a Person. I remind myself often that waking up in a new day is an invitation to begin again in dependence on the kindness of God, ordering my life in hopes of being present with Him.

Now let's take those questions you answered and consider our need to be reoriented to God's reality, live into God's design, and order life under God's wisdom.

Are you ready to learn more about God's desires for what a healthy you looks like? To grow in grace by surrendering all of life to God's good design over our attention, emotions, and limits? Let's begin.

SECTION I

A Healthy Life with God

"If you want to identify me, ask me not where I live, or what I like to eat, or how I comb my hair, but ask me what I think I am living for, in detail, and ask me what I think is keeping me from living fully the thing I want to live for. Between these two answers, you can determine the identity of any person. The better answer he has, the more of a person he is."[1]

—Thomas Merton

CHAPTER 1

Your Future Self

I WANT TO GIVE voice to the deep questions that are probably churning around in your heart. In all our hearts.

> Who do I want to be?
>
> What type of person should I become?
>
> Who am I now, and am I happy with who that person is?

The question underneath those remains: What am I living for?

Discipleship to Jesus is the continual surrender of all of life to God's good design for identity, belonging, and purpose.[1] We need to be reoriented to God's design and order for all of life under His wisdom.

REORIENTATION TO GOD'S REALITY

Before we know who to become, we must know what story we live in.[2] We all depend on a narrative to make sense of our experiences because life is confusing, hard, and beautiful all at once. I've known many people who have found their experiences too hard to bear so they try to escape life altogether. Some cope with socially acceptable (or unacceptable) addictions, make feelings their guide, or simply walk away from a faith never fully known. There is a reason strong leaders with a clear message gain crowds: we want purpose to make sense of the pain, so we look to someone willing to tell us a narrative that just might fit.

People throughout history have promised a way to the good life. Many of these older promises are still around, just in new wrapping. That new wrapping, in today's time, looks like social media, where the good life is constantly parading itself before our eyes. Scroll through Instagram, Facebook, or Amazon to see the promise of meaningful identity, belonging, and purpose found in materialism (I am what I have), consumerism (I am meant to acquire), perfectionism (I am what I do), rationalism (I am the final word), stoicism (I am unaffected by you), romanticism (I am my emotions), hedonism (I am my greatest pleasure), or postmodernism (I am what I say I am). These stories shape us early in life because before we name them, we feel them. They help us make sense of the world.

Which of these has lulled you into believing it might help you make sense of your life or bring fulfillment or happiness?

These stories are incomplete at best, and even a partial solution is insufficient for true life. Each story is a strategy to provide for yourself. Living in God's reality is as much about unlearning as it is about being remade, which is a kind of healthy deconstruction when things are rebuilt in God's design. The Scriptures tell of and invite us to consider the God-designed way of life. It is the one true story about all of life: who God is, who we are, and what we are to live for—in detail.

LIVING INTO GOD'S DESIGN

Life doesn't come custom ordered. You and I didn't choose where we were born or to what family of origin we belong. We didn't get to pick our childhood, our DNA, or our athletic build. The emotional health, maturity, and background of the people who raised us were preset for us. The values of our home, how we were taught the world worked, or the opportunities given to us—we all providentially received a life to do with the best we could. Everyone has a story, and our experiences are far from equal. Your character is grown by things you inherited, things done to you, things done around you, and the choices you made along the way in a fallen world.

In many ways, your personality is partly God-given (there are things that were just going to be true of you from the time you were in the womb), and at the same time, it is partly a complicated coping mechanism formed early in life as a means of survival.[3] You learned what kept you safe and accepted, helped you navigate emotions, or got you what you wanted. Over time these learned behaviors deeply affected your view of your own identity and eventually guided your strategies for obtaining the good life for yourself, and yet it is never enough. There's always more to us than the identity we've sought to cultivate in our own wisdom, and our Creator has always provided a better design.

How do we live in God's good design? Surrender. We defined discipleship earlier as continually surrendering all of life to God's good design for identity, belonging, and purpose. Now this may bring thoughts of passivity, but surrender is an active work. We are responsible for the effort of surrendering life to God while Christ has covered any need for earning through His generosity toward us. Living into God's design means that you *work out your own salvation* in daily life as you actively depend on "God who is working in you both to will and to work according to his good purpose" (Phil. 2:13).

Wait, you just said *work* three times in one sentence. I thought God was all about grace? If I'm not supposed to earn anything, what does that mean?

I love my children, and I care about who they become. If I don't train them how to live as functioning adults, I haven't done my job as their father, which is a selfish kind of love. My job is not to protect them from everything difficult in life. My job is to help them become the kind of person who can make good choices on their own. As they grow, I am present with them, guiding them, and at the needed moment, they have to pursue wisdom on their own. They have to work out what I've (hopefully) worked into them.

Life with God takes work, and it is work done *from* salvation, not *for* salvation. In Christ and empowered by the Holy Spirit, we work out what God has worked in as we surrender to His declaration of who He is, who we are, and what we should live for: Him.

BECOMING YOUR FUTURE SELF TAKES A LIFETIME

Becoming more like Christ is a lifelong process of actively depending on the Holy Spirit. It necessarily involves sowing toward the future version of ourselves, which means cultivating faith for right walking with God while resisting the ways the world seeks to form you. The future version of you that God has in mind is His child, fully human and fully alive, increasingly free of sin and shame, of insecurity and self-preoccupation. This future version is only possible in your surrender to Christ and union with Him.

The end goal is not that you become awesome; it's that you become truly human. With God, what you love—what guards and guides your attention, emotions, and limits—is set aright. The Christian life is a fight to live in reality at every turn, and the process of retraining our desires is one of constant friction. By retraining our loves to delight in God's design, we don't just try to sin less. We look to God and live more fully as we grow in wisdom.

But progress in the Christian life—growing in wisdom and becoming truly human—goes at a totally different pace than the speed of progress as defined by our surrounding culture. Think about it: the best-selling product of our contemporary world is daily life without friction. Instead of waiting or working on something, nowadays it's much simpler to buy, consume, or replace almost anything. Progress, for the world, brings fewer steps, burdens, clicks, and quicker outcomes.

When anything I can think of is available on my phone, it gets easier to expect character formation to be a one-click order with two-day shipping.

This drop-shipped character thinks authentic spiritual development is unrehearsed. If we had to plan to pray before we felt like praying or plan to read the Scriptures before we felt like doing so, it feels less than genuine. We wait for the right emotions to act rather than plan the actions that serve to order life (and our emotions) in God's wisdom.

But be honest with yourself. Do you treat any other area of life this way? Do you wait for the right feeling to complete tasks at work, or do you complete tasks so that you stay employed? How about laundry? I feel really inspired to wash clothes when the drawers are empty—so we do laundry *ahead* of no-sock day. What about counting calories or getting in a workout? Are these dependent on your fleeting emotions or delight in the idea of the future you that you want to become? What does it say about your view of God and growth in your walk with Him if many other things in your life get your effort even when you're not feeling it, but He doesn't? Could it be that you believe growth in those areas is actually more important?

Or, if it's easier for you to step away from your own life and look at another's, just think about the athletes you admire. Their accomplishments are rooted in disciplined pursuit of their goal. We praise athletes for their habitual dedication to their future self, and we struggle to connect the dots for the Christian life. The goal of the Christian life is for our minds to be renewed through a grace-fueled, Spirit-empowered, discipline-embracing way of life that necessitates our sustained effort.

Dallas Willard put it this way:

> The general human failing is to want what is right and important, but at the same time not to commit to the kind of life that will produce the action we know to be right and the condition we want to enjoy. This is the feature of the

> human character that explains why the road to hell is paved with good intentions.[4]

That one gets me every time. When it comes to following God's design for living, why is it so hard to follow through on my good intentions? Why can't I commit to the kind of life that will produce the action I know to be right and the condition I want to enjoy? The frictionless digital world trains us to believe that desires don't wait.[5] From a neurobiological angle, immediate gratification of our desires feels good because we get pleasure chemicals in our brain, even if minutes later we regret the decision. The quick impulse to obtain pleasure erodes our ability to delay gratification. We can't see any future moment besides this one.

Want an example of delayed gratification? Take Tom Brady, known for his year-round routine of self-discipline, which he admits is why he is able to be more than just another quarterback.[6] One writer comments that without Brady's ability to repeat monotonous, seemingly unimportant things on a daily basis, he would be "just another guy with big aspirations who couldn't live up to them," and that "when you're disciplined, with it also comes friction because you're not just doing what everyone else is doing."[7]

Now, of course, we need to make sure we aren't confusing the results with the means. If we think being more disciplined will make us more presentable before God, we're wrong. Spiritual discipline is not something that helps our future selves be more loved by God; rather, it is something that helps our future selves be more *surrendered to* Him.

The point is that if we want progress in the Christian life as God defines it—if we want to grow in wisdom and become truly human—we must get on board with the fact that becoming our future selves is a work of patient perseverance. The repetitive and continuous completion of actions and habits builds character, good or bad. Keep doing bad things, and you reap a bad character (Gal. 6:7). We know this is true from experience. We have all wanted to be better than we currently are in some category of life. And we've all seen the payoff of consistent, daily effort in that category. Spiritual growth is no different.

GETTING THE ORDER RIGHT

While sustained effort surely matters in our pursuit of spiritual maturity, as Christians we must pause and recognize that apart from Christ we are unable to change our fallen natures, even with the best of habits. We cannot change ourselves into new creations through building habits, developing virtue, or trying harder—we have to be born again first. Sinful humans can't change their natures or earn favor with God because sin is not merely something we do. We are born with a nature predisposed and inclined toward sin (Rom. 5).

It wasn't always that way. When God calls humanity good in Genesis 1:31, He means it. Adam and Eve are tempted by something outside themselves, while we are now tempted by our own internal evil desires (James 1:14). You and I came into the world after Genesis 3, and we have to be rescued out of our inborn inclination toward sin, our sinful actions, and the eternal consequences of sin against God. All of our faculties (mind, desires, actions) have been affected by sin, and therefore all of our faculties must be renewed through Christ.[8]

Only Christ can rescue us, and He doesn't ask us to change ourselves by having the perfect checklist of daily tasks or a track record of goodness before He saves us. He freely offers life and relationship through Himself first. *Then* He gives us the Holy Spirit to transform us into people who are increasingly able to do the things we are called to do: live in relationship with God and reflect His truth, goodness, and beauty in the world (Eph. 1:13–19; Rom. 12:2; Col. 3:1–17). This is why Jesus says we have to be born again (John 3:3) and why letter after letter in the New Testament shows the importance of ordering life as if we *actually believe* He will do what He says He will do.

God's will for the Christian is clear: be transformed into the image of your Maker (Rom. 12:2; Col. 3:10). But we must get the order right. First, we must become a new creature in our conversion to Christ, and only then can we act like this new creature. If you're a Christian, God has declared you to be a new creature, so exercise your new legs by training for godliness through the power of the Holy Spirit in you! Practice believing God will do as He says by living as He instructs, which includes consistent, purposeful effort in surrender, formation, and repentance.

THE GOAL OF GROWTH

So let's say you're a believer—a new creation—and you're committed to growing God's way, which you agree takes time and consistent effort. The natural next questions I often hear at this point are: "So, what is the goal of growth? What am I aiming toward?" The answer a lot of people assume is this: *sinning less.* The assumption is that the Christian life is about putting off sin, even against our greatest desires. Even when all our wants pull us in the opposite direction.

While we'll certainly have seasons where we resist temptation, I'd say that learning to resist all our bad wants is not the true goal of the Christian life. Living in God's reality is the true goal, which comes with God's ability to develop *new wants* inside our hearts.

For the Christian, it's not an issue of if we *can* put off our sin; it's an issue of if we *want* to put off our sin. We can blame others, find excuses, and easily distract our hearts from this truth. In the end, everybody makes choices and has to live with the consequences. You will choose based on what version of the good life you're chasing. Your desires drive your choices, and your desires *can change* when met with the grace of God. As we apply sustained effort toward our spiritual growth in cooperation with the Holy Spirit, He is able to help us not only choose and enact the right things but *desire* the right things at a heart level.

Have you ever thought:

> *But I want to put off my sin and it feels impossible!*
>
> *I keep trying and failing.*
>
> *God has to be disappointed with me. I'm so ashamed.*

We need the loud reminder of Scripture that there is "no condemnation for those in Christ" (Rom. 8:1). God isn't surprised by our weakness. Our recognition and remorse over our sin—the fact that we even *want* different desires—is a sign of the Spirit working in us, evidencing our union with Jesus. In other words, as we do what we can to shape the "outside" of our Christian lives with spiritual disciplines and sustained effort, the Holy Spirit shapes the "inside," and the gap between the two gets smaller and smaller until our outward living and our inner desires are united as one instead of divided.

With growth in the Christian life, think progress over perfection. Here's an example: One weekend you're doing yard work and get into a conversation with your neighbor Pete. He shares details of how life has been pretty hard and it's not getting better. In fact, Pete's wife has left him, and he's spent every night for the last six months trusting in alcohol to numb his hurts and avoid dealing with reality. You ask Pete if you could share about a time where you felt like you had no way forward but were able to find help for a better kind of life. You share Christ with Pete, and he responds with a desire to know more. Over the next month, Pete comes to believe in Jesus and recognizes the unhealthy pattern of his alcohol use is at odds with a life that flourishes with God.

Pete changes his route home from work and resolves to quit drinking. You can hear the hope in his voice. Pete is hungry to learn more about life with God. He goes three weeks without a single drink, and then Saturday morning Pete texts you about how one bad decision led to another after work yesterday. He woke up in someone else's bed, flooded with shame. Surely this proves his belief in Christ is fake; and if God is even real, He's surely more disappointed than before with Pete.

Christian, you cannot miss (or let Pete miss!) the work of Christ in his life for the twenty-one-plus days of health that came after six months of trying to escape reality. Change is slow, incremental, and often complicated because we are complex products of our choices, families of origin, emotional health, surrounding culture, and interpretations of life.

Something makes us feel like once we've been saved we're not allowed to be a mess anymore. To follow Jesus is to acknowledge you need help that you can't provide for yourself, but too many of us think that after we declare our neediness we shouldn't be needy! Jesus calls us to pursue holiness, which as I said before, we often take as sinning less instead of pursuing God's reality. When we walk in God's good design, sinning less is actually just the fruit of walking in wisdom.

Jesus is not surprised by your sin, and He does not shame you. He invites you forward! When you are tempted to cover your sin instead of admitting your need, it's no different from Adam and Eve hiding from God in the garden. The apostle Paul encourages us that Christ's past action has present implications for us through Romans 5:8: "God proves [present tense] his own love for us in that while we were still sinners, Christ died [past tense] for us."[9] For years I've heard my pastor offer the reminder: *all* your sins were future sins when Christ died for you. My sin is a surprise to me at times, but not to Jesus. He knows my need. And He's even more committed to transforming me into my future Christlike self than I am!

DISCUSSION QUESTIONS

1. How do you see the promise of a good life in our culture today? Why is this not the goal for the Christian?

2. What picture of your future self do you have in mind?

3. How have you tried to change yourself (specifically spiritually) in the past? Did it work? Was it lasting?

4. Before reading this chapter, what would you have said the goal of the Christian life is? How do you respond to "the goal of the Christian life is not only sinning less"? What, according to the author, is a better aim?

5. We are all becoming like somebody. If you haven't spent much time endeavoring to become more like Christ, who do you think you're becoming more like?

6. In what areas of life do you put daily, sustained effort? Why? What changes would be required for you to put sustained, daily effort into your spiritual growth?

7. What do you say you are living for? What does your life point to as to what you are living for? Are the two the same?

CHAPTER 2

Obstacles to Love and Growth

IN COLLEGE I GOT into a conversation about Christianity with a classmate. It's been twenty years, but I can still see the look on his face when I started to explain the worldview of the Bible. Christians believe in an invisible God who is three persons in one God. At the center of our faith is the belief that a virgin woman gave birth to a baby boy who is also the Son of God. Not only that, but the Bible informs us of invisible evil powers that are bent against God and those He loves, actively wielding shame, accusation, and lies to dishonor God through our actions. The Bible holds lots of fascinating things that are outside our daily experience.

Imagine the look on my classmate's face. He clearly believed I was the one who had embraced fiction and he had the grip on reality. My faith in the Bible was a fairy tale in his eyes. When it comes to his general outlook on reality, if he were ever to become a believer, he would have so many obstacles to overcome in the "miraculous things are actually possible in this world" department.

Many Christians assume that because we have agreed to the basic tenets of Christianity, our obstacles are dead and gone. But here's the truth: we have just as many obstacles. Perhaps they aren't obstacles to surrendering to God, but there are plenty of obstacles to *growing* in Him. And just like my classmate, they flow from our general outlook on who God is and His posture toward us.

For many of us, believing God is capable of miraculous things is not our holdup. After all, the concept of God, period, requires belief in the supernatural—in something outside this world. So it's not the idea of omnipotence or the supernatural we struggle with. For those trying to mature spiritually, I've found that instead of God being *able*, the most common obstacle to growth is actually whether God is loving, kind, and good.

This isn't just an obstacle I hear about; it's one I experience all the time myself. If asked, I'll tell you I believe God loves me like He says in the Scriptures *and* I struggle at times to believe that God is not just good for me but good to me.[1] I can also struggle to believe He is kind. Good can seem perfunctory, but kindness is what I long for—even if I'm afraid it's not true.

I know spiritual growth requires fresh experiences of forgiveness, but I struggle to receive forgiveness. I know consistently experiencing God's grace is crucial to spiritual maturity, but I tend to accept grace in theory but not in practice because "grace is for needy people" and I don't want to be needy. I'm bent to believe God's love is earned while He keeps proving it's freely given in the Son.

Do you struggle with any of these thoughts? The whisper under all of these fears is the accusation that God is not who He says He is when it comes to His goodness, kindness, and compassion.

But He *is* good, kind, and compassionate and a whole host of other attributes Scripture teaches us. To view Him any other way is to get our outlook on Him (and the world) wrong, just like my classmate did. If we see God wrongly, we deny ourselves the opportunity to receive forgiveness. If we believe love is dependent on performance, we will lie to ourselves about why things feel off. *If we get God wrong, we get life with Him wrong.*[2] If we view spiritual disciplines as performance for acceptance, we believe assumptions about God that are not true. When we see God rightly, we know how to show up each day in life with Him: beloved, in process, and on mission.

OBSTACLES TO SEEING GOD AS HE IS

It takes grace and effort to see God rightly.

Sin distorts our thinking and serves up shame on a daily basis about who we are; how God couldn't love us; and how if He or others knew the real us, they'd leave.

Many of us struggle with the obstacles of disbelief, skepticism, and cynicism, all of which are forms of protecting ourselves from being disappointed. Cynicism gets rewarded in many circles, because believing in the good seems naïve. Zack Eswine shares that "cynicism and skepticism keep us from embracing goodness and joy, and yet, here's the thing, cynicism can help you for a while. But it just can't get you through anything. Because any remedy that would ever come your way, you're going to doubt it. Because the one thing in life that you trust is your doubt."[3]

Along with cynicism, we often trust false promises of the good life more than Jesus. The scary thing is that these false promises deliver enough to get by but never what we truly need. Money can buy you comfort but not true joy. Fame can get you fans, but crowds bring trouble of their own. Perfectionism smooths the outside while you condemn yourself on the inside. Even as these narratives fail to fully deliver, we keep asking them to perform for us.

We struggle to trust God is good for us because we don't know our Bibles as well as we think, or we know we don't know the Bible so we avoid the Book and topic out of shame.

If skepticism, false promises, and shame aren't your hang-up in your journey toward spiritual maturity, the obstacle of busyness might be. Some of us are too busy doing things for Jesus to really know Jesus, settling for a conditional relationship where activity means acceptance. Jesus has no interest in this offer, but we convince ourselves it's what He really wants. It's the same move as the Galatians who began by faith and then depended on works (Gal. 2). We're welcomed in as children, yet through doubt and self-deception, tell ourselves we'll last longer if we act like hourly workers.

Finally, the most foundational obstacle many face is thinking of God as a father, let alone a *loving* father. Jesus seems safe to us because we can read His words and He walked the earth, but *Father*, that word is spring-loaded for many with emotion, fear, and doubt because of our earthly fathers.

If we get down to it, many people view God the Father as the angry, sin-hating God of the Old Testament and believe that Jesus Christ, God the Son, comes and dies in order to calm the Father down and take care of things.

This outlook on God comes when we've made Him in our image and not the other way around.

Do any of these obstacles resonate with you? Which one most obstructs your path as you journey toward maturity in your walk with God?

Throughout life we entrust ourselves (thoughts, emotions, desires) to other fallen human beings, who are largely unable to rightly handle their own emotions, let alone ours. We are loved, let down, cared for, hurt, abused, protected, disappointed, or nourished in these relationships. And then, for whatever reason, we take the bad experiences from the bunch and project them onto God. We expect God to handle us as poorly as others—with silence, disappointment, shame, explosive anger, or trying to fix things with trite Band-Aids when we have a gaping wound.

Do you base the love of God the Father on the failures of your earthly father? On the failures of your friends?

I believe the single most effective weapon against our joy in Christ and becoming who we are made to be is the lie that God is not who He says He is and you can't trust Him.

But if we take God at His Word, not our own, we hear a different reality. If we get this right, it will change our lives.

In John 15, Jesus tells His disciples: "As the Father has loved me, I have also loved you. Remain in my love" (v. 9).

Is this verse difficult to trust? It is often hard for me to believe Jesus means what He says here. I have plenty of objections to why God's love can't be that good, which are ways for me to protect myself from being disappointed if He really isn't.

But He is. We need our default scripts rewritten to see rightly.

"As the Father has loved me, I have also loved you. Remain in my love."

God does not love like we do. His love is better than ours and transforms us to be loved by Him and to love like Him.

Christian, we have moved not just from death to life, but God has reconciled us in *love*—from slave to sin to child of God.

You don't have to hang out by the door waiting to see if you're going to get invited in! You belong in God's house because it belongs to your heavenly Father; your older brother has a room ready for you. The Holy Spirit is at work in you to encourage and enable faith that God is who He says He is, and what He says about you is true. You don't have to live waiting for the other shoe to drop or worry you will wear out your welcome with God. His love for you isn't based on your ability to keep every rule. In fact, God's love for you has overcome your *inability* to keep every rule. Believe what He says and abide in His love. For only when you do this, believing what He says about who He is, will you be able to grow.

SEEING OURSELVES AS GOD SEES US

A professor friend of mine regularly asks his classes to write down the first thing that comes to mind when he says the word *humanity.*[4]

You try it. What comes to mind?

Using the same exercise, I have found the overwhelming response to this question is primarily negative. People say things like: sinful, broken, or messy. It's super cheery.

How you answer that question speaks to what you believe about humanity. There are two common thoughts in this discussion:

The first is that you and I are born with what we need to please God; we just need to try harder. You and I know what we should do; we're just lazy.[5] God knows what He's given us, and we're struggling to get it together, so He's disappointed with us. Again.

The second is we (with a good-intentioned humility) view ourselves as irreversibly broken, unable to do good, unlovable creatures. It is true that Adam and Eve (and you and I) were affected by sin in every faculty. This is described in the doctrine of total depravity. Many well-meaning people over apply this doctrine and live thinking it honors God to hate yourself. This makes us distrust that we can be loved "because there is nothing good in us," and the natural by-product is that we distance ourselves from God in our walk with Him.

When we believe this to be the core truth about ourselves, we view humanity from Genesis 3 instead of Genesis 1. Rather than hearing "very good," which was God's perspective on humanity before sin entered the picture, we look at ourselves (and others) as being only very broken. Yes, we're broken. The fall of man is real, and we live under its effects all day long. But this is simply not the whole picture.

If you've spent time in church, you've probably heard time and again that "all our righteous acts are like filthy rags" (Isa. 64:6 NIV), and none of them can earn God's favor. This is true. Outside of Christ, there is nothing in us that reconciles us to

God. The problem is when we think *we* are filthy rags. Instead of recognizing the impact of sin on our thoughts, emotions, and desires, we identify *as* our thoughts, emotions, and desires. Shame turns conviction over our actions into condemnation over our person.

If I believe that God sees me as irreparable and unlovable, I am trusting myself to tell me how God views me, which affects all of life. When we listen to the accusation that we are filthy rags, we ignore the arc of the entire Bible that points to our triune God who made humanity in His image, loves them—loves us—and has a plan to restore us.[6] When the first descriptor we consider about people is *sinful* instead of *loved*, we reinforce accusations of shame and unworthiness (that are not from God) and find ourselves trying to earn acceptance with God when it has been given to us in Jesus.

If you are in Christ, the Bible says you are not just "sinner"; you are *saint*, and God has plans to make you "very good" again. The Bible also says your shame is taken away *forever* (Rom. 8). You're united to Christ and cannot be snatched from Him. The Holy Spirit is in you. Satan will accuse you, cast doubt on God's character, on God's work in your life, and promise you actually can provide for yourself. *It's the same move he made in the garden*, and if you don't pay attention, these attacks will steal your hope.

We readily believe that no habit or act can earn us favor with God, but when we're stressed or shamed, our default move is to *try harder* at being good. We act on a deep suspicion that God is not as good as He says He is. If we let God define who He is, we resist the urge to make Him into the image of people who have failed us. This makes all the difference, clearing the obstacles to love and rooting ourselves in God's reality.

Life with God is not merely about saving you from the punishment or presence of sin. Life with God is about being reconciled to your Maker and becoming a certain type of person who desires to dwell in God's presence, demonstrate His care over creation, and image His beauty to the world.

Christian, you are invited in as a beloved child.

God is who He says He is, and what He says about you is true. He really is not just omnipotent but *good,* and you are not just sin-stricken but *loved.* Only when you believe this whole picture of both *God* and *you* can you start growing in spiritual maturity.

And when you hear the lies start rolling in, remind yourself of this: if God the Father hated you, the *person*, He wouldn't have sent His Son to save you, His Son wouldn't have volunteered to do the job, and His Spirit wouldn't dare indwell you. But He did, and He did, and He did. Indeed, God hates your sin. He hates what you're infected with, and He's committed to pulling it out of you. Because He loves *you,* the person, who is made in His image. He is more committed than you could ever know to transform you back into the picture of what it once looked like to be human without the cancer of sin. And that's a gloriously *good* picture.

Take some time now to thank God for His generosity to you and the fact that He is not just good for you but good *to* you—and He is kind.

DISCUSSION QUESTIONS

1. We're all walking down a path toward spiritual maturity, and the author makes the case that we encounter two kinds of obstacles as we journey down this path: obstacles in our belief about *who God is* and obstacles in our belief about *who we are.* Would you say you have more obstacles in the former or the latter category?

2. What are the various obstacles we encounter when it comes to our view on who God is? Outside of those explored in this chapter, have you experienced any other obstacles in your context? Which is most difficult for you to overcome?

3. Why is it so crucial for us to allow God to tell us who He is as seen in Scripture, instead of our culture, circumstances, or feelings telling us who He is?

4. What are the various obstacles we encounter when it comes to our view on who we are? Which one most resonated with you, and why?

5. How do you generally imagine God feeling about you? Why? Why is it so crucial for you to trust Scripture to define His posture toward you instead of your feelings or imagination?

6. Why is true growth in God contingent upon a right view of Him and a right view of self? How is growth inhibited when we get one of these wrong?

7. How does it change things to know that God deemed humanity "very good" before sin entered the picture? How does this give you hope for your growth journey?

CHAPTER 3

Why a Spiritually Disciplined Life Feels Difficult

I GREW UP IN a Baptist church with red carpet and white Corinthian columns. As a teen, my grasp of church history was pretty limited. I didn't know much of what happened between the New Testament, Monty Python's search for the holy grail, and Billy Graham crusades. The first time I heard the Apostles' Creed may have been from Rich Mullins.

Twenty-five years after that *Ragamuffin* CD, I've come to appreciate the history of our faith and many of what Dallas Willard calls "old things recently forgotten."[1] In our journey toward a future self that flourishes with God, we must know what happened in the past, for if we ignore all that lies behind us, we abandon a host of wisdom for life in our day and beyond. Said another way, when we take the time to explore the waters upstream from our moment in time, we'll realize why the rapids downstream, where we live, feel so intense. History, as it turns out, isn't just a subject or a hobby; it is strongly shaping many experiences in our daily lives, including our spiritual disciplines (or lack thereof).

What I'm getting at is this: there's a reason you find spiritual disciplines hard in our present-day culture. On one hand, being spiritually disciplined is difficult for any human born after the fall. That's been true no matter what land or time you live in because the same seeds of sin live inside all of us. On the other hand, living a spiritually disciplined life is *especially* hard for you right now, given past ideas and their far-reaching consequences—consequences that are at play in almost every moment of your daily life. They are shaping you, which includes your spiritual life. So let's briefly explore them so that you're more prepared to recognize when they are warring against your walk with God.

WAKING UP DOWNSTREAM

For most of the last two thousand years, the God of the Bible was viewed by Western civilization as the source of life-orienting truth. God is external to us, objectively true, in control of His creation.

If we take a quick look around our culture now, it's clear that God is no longer considered this source of life-orienting truth.

What happened? Considering the pendulum swings of Christian and secular thought throughout time helps make sense of the cultural waters we woke up in, so let me paint the picture for you in broad brushstrokes (and please grant me forgiveness for oversimplicity, for the task of summing up history almost always cuts out nuance).

From the early church to the medieval period, the best-case scenario for the Christian was "life in God's good design and union with Christ." In medieval times this narrative moved from "flourishing in God's design" to "God is angry with us and our sin so we must pay penance to prove we're sorry." Then, finally, in the Protestant Reformation the narrative became "salvation by faith in Christ alone, not penance."[2]

Within three centuries, the authoritative basis for culture aggressively shifted from *external, objective* truth (i.e., "I didn't make myself, and I trust the wisdom of my Creator") toward an *internal, subjective* truth ("I trust my own reason to know what is best, and I owe my allegiance and behavior to no one"). The flood of philosophy and science that followed predominantly elevated humankind's authority over their own lives, and by the twentieth century, divine revelation had been unseated by the scientific method as the basis of authoritative truth.

We see the effects to this day, especially in the West. Our posture toward truth in America has continued to champion what we see, feel, and experience as the ultimate reality. Now the authoritative truth of our moment is not what we can replicate but what we feel is best. We choose our beliefs, our identities, our loves, our truth because *choice is freedom*. Every aspect of our humanity is now culturally liberated and regulated to individual freedom of choice.

Impacted by nearly a century of marketing, our choices are flooded, nudged, and formed by upwards of ten thousand advertisements a day—all aimed at our desires, not our rational self.[3]

In short, we're living in a cultural moment where the promise of choice has shaped us as consumers instead of creatures. We define ourselves by our choices, and our choices are driven by our desires. Our desires drive the economy because *frugality and contentment aren't virtues within a consumer society*.[4]

What does this all have to do with our spiritual growth, you ask? Or spiritual disciplines? It has everything to do with it. For when we try to pray, we fidget, get discouraged, or glance at our phone for something that feels like productivity, comfort, or distraction. When we try to read our Bibles for an extended amount of time, we don't get to enjoy the flood of pleasure chemicals the Internet gives us when we offer it the same amount of our time. When we must sacrifice something for God or for our family, it feels like oppression on our autonomy or freedom instead of the obvious path to strong relationship. This is the lifeblood of our brave new world: keep moving, keep soothing, keep spending, and avoid the weight of reality.

When our identity is our choice and authenticity our value, we delight in ourselves more than our Creator. And how do we delight in a Creator whose authority, goodness, and kindness we question?

Many of us treat life with God as a task to complete instead of a person to know and be known by. In efforts to learn about God, we focus on the *how* of our salvation at the expense of knowing the *who* that has come toward us in Christ. Without a deep look at the *who* of our Savior (the incarnate Son who reveals the heart of the Father), we focus on *how* we are saved. Longing for wholeness and looking for action, we depend on mechanics instead of Christ Himself.

Think about the question I asked you earlier: Who do you want to become? What identity have you created for yourself, and how much of your individual expression might be the result of someone else's marketing? What are you trusting to bring meaning to your soul outside of the life-orienting truth of your Creator?

As many have said, we become what we behold. What do we behold these days outside of constant advertisements and algorithm-driven reinforcement of our preferences?

Christian, behold Jesus, because He reveals the Father (John 14; Col. 1). Our self-focused scripts need to delight in who our Savior is as He reveals the heart of His Father. Beholding Christ renews our desires and clarifies the true choice: delighting in our Maker or delighting in ourselves. Life with God integrates our design and desires instead of fragmenting them. With right belief in the how of our faith, we learn we are loved by seeing *who* has saved us. Seeing *who* rightly fuels our response to His love through the *what* we practice in daily life. We are to become a certain kind of person, which means we must be purposeful in who (and what) we repeatedly behold.

THE TENSION OF DISCIPLINE

In all those years between the New Testament and tent revivals, Christians trained their hearts (mind, desires, actions) to be present with God through the practice of intentional disciplines. By repeated grace-driven effort, these actionable habits help direct our attention, emotions, and limits toward God in daily life.

A few foundational historical disciplines are Bible-reading, prayer, evangelism, sabbath, fasting, and generosity. They are practices of both engaging in and abstaining from, training and disciplining our desires toward godliness. These practices make space for us to be attentive to God.

About five hundred years before and during the time Jesus walked the earth, there was a consensus in culture when it came to how a person could train their character: the pursuit of virtue (courage, friendship, modesty, patience, etc.). Aristotle believed people could practice virtues and seek the midpoint (or mean) between having too little or too much of any one character trait.[5] It's like working on getting your blood work numbers in the right range, but for your soul. These virtues then were a type of embodied harmony between your mind, desires, and actions.[6] (For example, the "mean" or "middle" between being rash and being cowardly was the virtue of *bravery*. Or the middle ground between being stingy and being frivolous is the virtue of *generosity*.)

Seeing these as *habituated ways of being*, Aristotle believed these virtues enabled people to possess the good life. They constructed a self-based happiness and ordered life to that end. The goal became finding and sustaining the mean, the middle ground, in all things.

To make sure you don't hear what I'm not saying: Aristotle does not account for the biblical understanding of sin, need for salvation, or God's provision for humankind. The mean of the Christian life is solely found through the center cross of Christ.[7] The believer in Christ has been united with Christ by faith in His merit, not ours. We are no longer concerned with being *good enough* for God to love us. We order life under His good design *because* He loves us and rescues us from sin, Satan, and death while we are busy rebelling against Him (Rom. 5). Life, then, is to abide in Christ's teaching as the Spirit renews us from the inside out, enabling us to pursue holiness in our mind, desires, and actions (John 15; Col. 3).

Closer to Aristotle than Christ, our culture largely values image over substance. A chief offender here is celebrity culture, which teaches that we simply need to *appear* to be a certain kind of person. It's a world of "fake it 'til you make it," where pretending takes far less effort than becoming the person we portray ourselves to be. Let me post the curated, filtered view of my life—a vacation, award, date night, new house, car, or workout—and I get rewarded with likes for what I leave out. In our social hearts, the thought of celebrity has eclipsed the hope of character. Cicero talked about this when he said, "Few are those who wish to be endowed with virtue rather than to seem so."

Shortcuts to character are tempting. We look for the path of least resistance in all areas of life. I scan every checkout line for which is shortest because I am in a hurry. Valuing speed, we regularly make choices that go against our slower ideals. After all, who wants to develop their ability to wait? Who wants to willingly choose environments that cultivate a character trait like patience? We can blame it on the day or a lack of willpower, but we choose against our future selves all the time.

I repeatedly tell my kids: people make choices, and choices have consequences—good or bad.

Christians obviously do not offer allegiance to Aristotle, but we do take note that he stumbled upon something that, ultimately, he can't really take credit for, and that is the power of intentional, repeated habits. Indeed, God Himself wove this truism into the human experience, for godly, regular habits play a key factor in becoming who we were made to be. That was true in the daily and weekly rhythms God asked His people to practice in the Old Testament, and it's true for New Testament believers today as we practice various spiritual habits that shape us into Christ's image. When we practice regular biblical rhythms and disciplines, we direct our whole selves to be present to God, and in God's presence we are changed over time. Holding onto the truth that *grace is opposed to earning, not effort,* we can work out our salvation by putting on the new self, knowing all our efforts are carried by the indwelling Spirit of God[8] (Phil. 2:12; Eph. 4:24).

Many of us struggle to delight in spiritual disciplines because of an overpromised or underexpected understanding of what to hope for in these moments. Based on what you value, you will expect different results from rhythms of life with God.

Life with God is a series of tensions to be held in balance. Our disciplines must be strategic **and** allow for spontaneity.[9] Every relationship thrives on structure and surprise. We are meant to become a fully formed self, **and** we only become so in the presence of another. We are justified through faith alone in Christ alone, **and** it is our *being*—who we become—that we offer to Jesus in glory.[10] God will complete the work He has started in us, **and** He calls us to actively participate in the forming of our character (Phil. 1:6; Titus 2:7; 1 Tim. 6:18; Rom. 8:28; 2 Cor. 9:8; Col. 3). Depending on your faith tradition, you may need to hear that life with God has **both** objective truth **and** subjective experience. We live with God's revealed Word, **and** the indwelling Holy Spirit is alive and well within the people of God.

When out of balance, any one of these leads to error. Spiritual disciplines form and maintain both our individual and corporate identity. The power of transformation is not in the discipline itself but in the continual turning to God and being changed by the Spirit over time.

If we expect every sit-down with the Bible to be a burning-bush moment, we miss the compounding effect of daily orienting our mind, emotions, and actions toward God as the keeper of reality. If we never expect to meet the Spirit of God in the Scriptures, we will miss the invitation to remove our shoes, passing by holy ground. If worship in song is centered on how I feel about God, I miss the opportunity to be confronted with a God not of my own making. Likewise, if I continually expect to be shamed for my failures, I miss the invitation to worship God in freedom. We all need to be reminded of His beauty and love. God is more than your preferences and tradition. If you're never surprised by His grace or confronted by His love, I'd make sure you're worshipping the God of the Bible.

Spiritual disciplines are a long game, fought daily by training our hearts (mind, desires, and actions). It takes humility to be disciplined, and discipline is key to becoming a disciple of Jesus. We live in an anti-authority age, each of us an authority to ourselves. The disciplines are helps for *us*, not Him—we are the ones whose memory is like a bottomless bucket. The disciplines make space for our hearts to be reoriented to God's reality.

One last tension before we move on: God deals with you in gentleness.

God gives us Himself at great cost to Himself. The Father, Son, and Spirit aren't out to shame us into right living; God invites you into life as He designed it to be. He invites you to become who He made you to be so that you can enjoy His goodness in all things.

Trust that God is gentle toward you, and then be gentle with yourself. Christian, do you receive gentleness from God and then shame yourself? God's not condemning you. Christ Himself said He reveals the Father (John 14) and that He is gentle in heart (Matt. 11). He is inviting you to live in reality. Stop listening to accusations of shame. (Who are they coming from, anyway?) "By this we shall know that we are of the truth and reassure our heart before him; for whenever our heart condemns us, God is greater than our heart, and he knows everything" (1 John 3:19–20 ESV).

You will succeed *and* fail. Embracing life as an ongoing process of becoming helps us get back up again. There is no success without failure, and every awareness of need is an invitation to keep moving forward in grace.

TODAY SHAPES TOMORROW

You and I are the product of the choices we made in all our yesterdays. If you asked me to change who I am right now, there is little I could do. My past choices have shaped how I'll react to this moment. If I want to change how I respond in a future moment, I have to *discipline* myself toward the future me.

This is good news, for it means we have immense influence over who we are a year from now. It means that though the movements of history are behind us, shaping us in strong ways, the days ahead of us can look different if we want them to. It all hinges on what or whom we love. We are capable of doing incredible things to get what we want or be with those we love. The problem is that we want the God-designed quality of life, but we fail to discipline ourselves to have a fighting chance at lasting change.

The strange thing about the Christian life is that you don't mature by working harder on yourself for Jesus. You mature by focusing on Jesus and looking away from yourself. What we love shapes who we become, and as our fallen loves have turned us inward, we need to be turned out toward God. The transformed and renewed Christian mind understands itself *outside of the self.*[11] As we center our attention, emotions, and limits on Jesus (which we'll talk about in the next section of the book), the Spirit of God does the work by enabling us to love rightly.

Therefore, "not only do we know God through Jesus Christ alone; but we know ourselves only by Jesus Christ."[12] We need the Spirit of God to retrain our disordered loves so that we love God, ourselves, and others rightly. We are creatures carried along by our loves, and our loves need to be renewed and reordered in the image of our Creator.

As someone who *loves* learning, let me encourage you: life with Christ involves learning over time. Don't let *what* you don't yet know distract you from *who* is for you now. Our hope is a living person, and our mind, desires, and actions follow Him based on our trust of *who* He is, not understanding every detail of *what* He's done. *If we would be assured that God is pleased with and kindly disposed toward us, we must fix our eyes on Christ alone.*[13]

This is the soil we want to root our lives: ordering our days in God's wisdom and presence, actively depending on the Holy Spirit to become who we were made to be.

DISCUSSION QUESTIONS

1. The author made the case that, in previous centuries, the common outlook on life was that God's design governed

humanity. Then history moved toward a more self-focused authority. In what ways do you see this playing out in our culture? In what ways do you see it playing out in your daily life?

2. Do you consider yourself a disciplined person? Why or why not?

3. Before reading this book, what was your opinion on intentional, repeated habits? Has your perspective changed? How so?

4. What are some ways you actively avoid developing certain character traits? Why do you think you do this?

5. Read the text by Jonathan Edwards on the following pages. How does this point you to the *who* of our faith? How does it reveal the beauty of God?

6. Like a gardener tending to the tree of our life, we do all we can to cultivate a life that flourishes as the Spirit of God works the growth. How would you describe your spiritual life today? Is it flourishing? Does it need tending?

7. When you envision a future version of yourself, spiritually speaking, what do you see? What changes do you need to make today to shape this picture of tomorrow?

Interlude: Christ Is to the Heart like a River to a Tree Planted by It

Jonathan Edwards, 1742

He shall be like a tree planted by the rivers of water. (Ps. 1:3 KJV)

For he shall be as a tree planted by the waters, and that spreadeth out her roots by the river, and shall not see when heat cometh, but her leaf shall be green; and shall not be careful in the year of drought, neither shall cease from yielding fruit. (Jer. 17:8 KJV)

The glorious LORD will be unto us a place of broad rivers and streams. (Isa. 33:21 KJV)

DOCTRINE

Christ is to the heart of a true saint like a river to the roots of a tree that is planted by it.

In the following respects:

I. As the waters of a river run easily and freely, so the love of Christ. He freely came into the world. He laid down his life and endured those dreadful sufferings.

His blood was freely shed: blood flowed as freely from his wounds as water from a spring.

All the good things that Christ bestows on his saints come to them as freely as water runs down in a river.

The chief and most excellent things that Christ bestows are the influences of his Spirit on their hearts, to enlighten and sanctify and comfort.

These all come freely from Christ, like the waters of a river.

Christ willingly gives his people, that look to him and trust in him, light and life in their souls.

II. Christ is like a river in the great plenty and abundance of his love and grace.

The love of Christ is great, and he has done great things from love.

The good things that are the fruits of his love are infinitely great.

The happiness that he gives is worth more than all the silver and gold in the world.

The tree that spreads out its roots by a river has enough water: no need for rain or any other water.

So the true saint finds enough in Christ: great plenty of water—enough to supply a great multitude of persons with drink to satisfy all their thirst. There is enough to supply the roots of a multitude of trees; so, for all saints.

III. Waters of a river don't fail; it flows constantly, day and night.

Waters that run upon the ground from showers of rain or melting of the snow soon dry up, but waters from rivers do not.

Little brooks dry up in a very dry time, but the waters of a great river continue running, continually and from one age to another, and are never dry.

So Christ never leaves his saints that love him and trust in him: the love of Christ never ceases.

He never leaves off to take care of them.

The grace of Christ in the heart shall always continue. Christ never will take away his Spirit from them: that inward life and comfort that Christ gives the hearts of his saints shall continue to all eternity.

When death comes, that comfort and happiness shall continue.

When the end of the world comes, yet their comforts shall still be like a river that shall not be dried up.

IV. A tree planted by a river is never dry: so Christ is never exhausted.

The soul of the saint is joined to Christ and they are made one.

As the water enters into the roots of the tree, so Christ enters the heart and soul of a godly man and dwells there.

The Spirit of Christ comes into the very heart of a saint as water to the roots of a tree.

V. Water refreshes; so Christ refreshes and satisfies the heart, and makes it rejoice.

Water gives life and keeps it alive; so Christ enlivens the heart and makes it grow: makes it grow beautiful and fruitful.

A tree planted by a river is green in time of great drought, when other trees wither.

So the soul of a true saint is sustained by Christ in time of affliction, at death and even at the end of the world.

APPLICATION

I. Examine whether you are a true saint.

Has your soul ever been like a tree planted by this river?

They that are saints have been the subjects of a great change: their souls are like a tree digged up by the roots out of a dry, barren ground, and planted in a new place. Their hearts are taken off from this world and planted in God and Christ and heaven: they no more trust in the world, but put their trust in God. They do not trust in themselves, their own strength or righteousness, but trust only in Christ.

If you are a saint, then Christ is sweet and refreshing to you, as the water of a river to a man when he is very thirsty.

Is Christ sweeter and better than the sweetest food, better than all the things of the world?

Has your mind been enlightened to see that there is enough in Christ?

Does your religion continue like a tree planted by a river, or does your religion come to nothing, like a tree planted in a dry, barren ground?

The religion of a worldly man is like puddles after a rain that soon dry up.

But the religion of a truly good man is like a river.

Do you bring forth fruit?

II. Sinners, seek an interest in Jesus Christ. If you are not in Christ, though you may be like green trees, yet by and by you will wither.

All your streams will fail you.[1]

SECTION II

THREE DIMENSIONS FOR A HEALTHY LIFE WITH GOD

DIMENSION ONE

Disciplining Our Attention

Choruses from "The Rock," I.

T. S. Eliot

The Eagle soars in the summit of Heaven,
The Hunter with his dogs pursues his circuit.
O perpetual revolution of configured stars,
O perpetual recurrence of determined seasons,
O world of spring and autumn, birth and dying!
The endless cycle of idea and action,
Endless invention, endless experiment,
Brings knowledge of motion, but not of stillness;
Knowledge of speech, but not of silence;
Knowledge of words, and ignorance of the Word.
All our knowledge brings us nearer to our ignorance,
All our ignorance brings us nearer to death,
But nearness to death no nearer to GOD.

Where is the Life we have lost in living?
Where is the wisdom we have lost in knowledge?
Where is the knowledge we have lost in information?
The cycles of Heaven in twenty centuries
Bring us farther from God and nearer to the Dust.

CHAPTER 4

Dethrone the Digital Savior

EACH FALL I TEACH high schoolers about Jonathan Edwards and George Whitefield, both renowned preachers in their day. Given that we're talking about preachers and preaching, I ask the students about their experience of church and when the sermon starts to hit a little too close to home.

What happens at the point when our attention is drawn to God's truth and we start to feel displeased with ourselves in light of it? What do we do when Scripture forces us to look in the mirror to self-examine and we don't like what we see?

Enter the functional savior who helps us avert our eyes and offer our attention elsewhere: the digital world and its many distractions. Open an app, and the buzz of anticipation saves us from the pain of discomfort. Our phones promise to relieve us of our negative emotions, removing friction so we can glide on unhindered by that pesky human instinct called introspection. As a culture, we have welcomed the ever-present nature of technology into our lives. Ever thought: *How did my phone get in my hand?* Maybe these moments are intentional. Either way, our habitual return to the digital world shows we functionally abide in technology rather than in Christ.[1] The message is clear: *no need to feel conviction—here's unending novelty wrapped in dopamine to ease your mind.*

Digital distraction is not only a constant pull on our attention, but it is the most agenda-driven and culturally pervasive factor we freely welcome into our modern lives. If your life feels dominated by work, your kids' sports schedules, making lunches, cleaning house, sitting in class—what do you do when you need a break from the moment? Same thing you might do in church when the Word of God goes to work: you reach for a digital fix. Just as the addict runs to the substances of nicotine, sugar, or alcohol to numb the sting of stress or pain (and then eventually just runs to the substance *whenever* because the habit has become entrenched in his daily rhythms), we all—each one of us—seek pleasure on demand from tiny screens and heart buttons. If we're honest, we not only do this in hard moments from which we want escape but in *any* moment. Even the fun ones. Even the meaningful ones. Our attention is *that* disoriented.

Why? Because we give our attention to what we delight in. Our attention is the most precious commodity we have. It is worth billions of dollars *every day* to companies who want to monetize our moments, desires, and good intentions. This is the attention economy. It wants to distract you from real life, shape who and what you love, and track it all in an ever-improving algorithm for the next moment you are stressed, tired, lonely, or simply acting on impulse. Take a scroll break—you'll feel better.

Over time, abiding in tech is less about your freedom of choice and more about falling prey to an increasingly perfected trap. (Even those who first worked to engineer digital addiction admit to the "trap setting" now—they are warning others about its detriments).[2] Our natural vulnerability has been used against us. The digital bait turns our thoughts, emotions, and actions into profit. We are primarily seen as a *product*, not as a being created in the image of God. The true cost of these free platforms is the diminishing ability to enjoy life with God and bear His image in life with others.[3]

Being made in God's image in not about what we should or should not do. Instead, God's image calls us to become the kind of person who can delight in what is true, good, and beautiful. You are meant to enjoy life with delight that reflects God's glory.

Just so we're clear, I'm not hammering this out on a typewriter in my barn.

Not yet.

When we give away our attention for the reward of distraction, we forfeit the quiet moments of our lives that we need to hear God. It's hard to cultivate awareness to God, self, and others when staring at a screen.

If we want to become healthier Christians—if we want to become that future self who looks more like Christ—the first major area of life in which we need to be spiritually disciplined is our *attention*. Or said more specifically, what we do with the gift of our attention. How are we stewarding moments with our families, communities, and our workplace? How do we view time alone? Is it time to think, or is our default to check in on our digital worlds? The addiction loops we share with our tech habits keep us checking in somewhere else instead of joining in on what we're divinely invited into. We have an eternal purpose, and it's not measured in likes.

My guess is that, when it comes to spiritual disciplines, you already know you should be doing the obvious things like reading your Bible more, sharing the gospel, praying, giving, and the like. The reason you don't move toward those spiritual habits isn't because you don't think they are important—or even because you can't find a book to help you do them better. It's because your attention is compromised. It's because there are some preliminary disciplines you haven't put in place to make space for the obvious ones.

So, how do we reclaim and retrain our attention? How might we offer up our attention to God instead of all other distractions?

We discipline ourselves to do three things: *dethrone the digital savior, cultivate a transformed heart,* and *learn to listen*. In the remainder of this chapter, we'll consider some spiritual habits to help us do the first of these three, and then in the following pages (chapters 5 and 6), we will explore the other two.

DETHRONE THE DIGITAL SAVIOR

Typically when I get frustrated with the amount of time I spend on my phone, I delete the offending apps, block the Internet, and vow to do better. At some future point, to make sure I haven't missed a message, need to look something up, or add to the shopping cart—it's good intentions out, app store in.

It's not that bad, right? Maybe not, if we're talking about one-off experiences. But if I really think about it, it's the cumulative effect of these moments I often miss. My kids repeatedly calling my name until I finally hear them, my wife going silent on date night because I checked my phone while she was talking, or the embarrassment (and resentment) I feel when I get honked at while scrolling news at the red-turned-green light. These moments are actively forming me *and* speaking to the people around me: "What's in the glowing rectangle is more important than here, now, *you*."

Few of us would say, *I trust my digital world to save me from my sins.*

That would be ridiculous.

And yet how many times a day do we ask our device to deliver us from every other existential crisis?

Our culture has become dependent on our devices to the point their absence brings anxiety. Strangely, the visible presence of a device also distracts from the moment. A 2020 study of Instagram users cited the increasingly compulsive draw to share details of daily life. It started innocently, but then, "In my head, whenever I was doing anything I was thinking 'what can I share online?' I was obsessed . . . if there was an occasion or event [I] was thinking already: 'how am I going to put this on social media?'"[4]

Ever caught yourself thinking not about how you could best *enjoy* a moment but how you could best *share* that moment online?

Me too.

If we want the life God offers, we cannot treat the digital space like our savior from boredom. It must simply be a tool for daily life. Technology is not neutral, and it's here to stay. How we steward it in our lives is one the most pressing discipleship issues for Christians today. If we fill our down moments with the delight of tech, we are in real danger of crowding out space to hear God's voice in daily life.

DISCIPLINES TO PRACTICE

If we're going to dethrone our digital savior in order to, instead, give our attention to God, we need some disciplines to start building habits that enable pursuit of what we actually want: a Christ-formed character. Here are three disciplines you can begin practicing today.

1. Fast from digital environments.

For a period of time each week, try to live life like you don't have the Internet or a phone. Give yourself this space to look up instead of down. Turn your phone off for part of the day, or one day a week, or in airplane mode to be present to the moment.

When we voluntarily deprive ourselves of something, we create space to pay attention to our lives. When we fast from food, we remind ourselves that our fellowship with God is true food for our souls. When we fast from digital connection, we are reminded of the beauty within embodied relationships. We value presence with our people over disembodied notifications. Be your own person, know what you like because *you* like it, not because the algorithm encourages you to. What slice of time each week could you dedicate to fasting? To looking up?

2. Create meaningful friction.

Necessity is the mother of invention, which means technology relieves the burden of necessity by promising "to bring the forces of nature and culture under control, to liberate us from misery and toil, and to enrich our lives."[5] Good ideas make hard things easier. At this point in history, we're not looking to make hard things easier so much as to make daily life effortless.[6]

A life free of burden and built on ease is not a flourishing Christian life. Technology is built on access, convenience, and fewer steps to checkout. Christianity comes with denial of self that God is honored in our minds, emotions, and actions. Technology enables faster fulfillment of our desires. Christians discipline their compulsions by inserting friction to mature our desires. Just because we want it and can buy it, doesn't mean we should. The scrolling only refreshes; we have to opt out. Here are a few suggestions to help you create a little more friction.

One, put your digital tools into appropriate domains. Allow whatever is necessary to live on your phone. Allow what is helpful or *asked of you* (but not necessary) to live only on your computer. Leave access to compulsive tools either on a commonly held device (like a family computer), or just take them off computers and phones entirely. For example, if the ability to call or text your child is necessary for their pickup and drop-off schedules, allow this access on your phone. If your job asks you to be conversant on social media, news, or email—okay, but leave access to those things on your computer, not in your pocket. I could go on, but I think you get the gist. This practice removes the temptation to passively consume from your phone (or smart watch). Our compulsions can catch us at any moment, so create friction to be present in your life.

Two, defend your vulnerabilities ahead of time. In another study of eighteen- to thirty-five-year-olds, 41 percent used some type of control to access apps on their phones. I've used one of these apps for years because I know there are moments and seasons where my restless anxiety is stronger than my will. As one thinker would put it: "Now that we can satisfy almost any desire from the comfort of our own homes, very often we must decide *not* to do something rather than to do it."[7] We are all capable of sabotaging our work, our relationships, and our holiness by wasting attention on the wrong things. Don't wait until you're in the throes of compulsion. To protect your vulnerabilities, limit your usage on the front end by adjusting your settings (or downloading certain tracking apps). It's much harder to say no in the heat of the digital pull than it is to prepare for the heat to come.

3. Be spiritually expectant.

What's the draw of tech? Novelty. Where daily life can feel monotonous or boring, an endless stream of new things introduces surprise and anticipation into our days. When we lose the expectation that reality will reward our attention, we escape into the digital. We are digitally expectant.

How many of us are waiting on the Lord in our daily lives like this? How many of us are as spiritually expectant as we are digitally? Are we so distracted and conformed by the world that we live entitled to entertainment rather than expecting to encounter God? Rather than live through a screen, we have the opportunity to cultivate beauty through our embodied presence. We can actively pray and expect that He hears and responds to His children.

Here's how you could practice spiritual expectancy:

- **Each morning, pray through the day (and the faces) ahead.** Consider each routine, appointment, meeting, commute, car line, meal, bedtime, or chore. Think of people you will interact with—family, children, coworkers, educators, baristas, wait staff—and pray for them by name. Pray for the presence of mind to see others you encounter as people made in the image of God and not simply the provider of your coffee or driver in your way. Broaden your focus and consider how you might encourage or minister to them.
- **When you are with others, be present.** Reclaim the ability to be present to those

you are with by disciplining your digital compulsions. Build meaningful connection that trumps the itch for your phone. Proactively engage and resist the urge to check in elsewhere. (This may require leaving your phone in your car or turning it off during an outing.)

- **Expect God to answer prayer.** When you pray, know that God hears and responds. He has specifically placed you to image His character to the people who see your life in person, not merely in posts. Be open to God's interrupting you with invitations to join His work.
- **Catch and release your compulsions.** When you are tempted to expect more out of the digital than your physical life, get curious about why. You are not your thoughts, but you are responsible for your actions. Give yourself a few minutes to hold your thoughts and bring them to God in prayer. Tell Him when the compulsions rise up. Listen for how He responds.

DISCUSSION QUESTIONS

1. How do you find your attention drawn to the digital world? In what environments are you most tempted to engage it as a distraction or escape?

2. When you reach for technology, what are you hoping it will relieve you of? Boredom? Discomfort? Silence? Sadness? Anger? Why do you think tech is a better rescuer from these things than God is?

3. What impact on your presence to God, yourself, and others do your devices have in daily life? Which people are most harmed by your lack of presence and attention?

4. Do you think the digital world can be treated as a tool for your growth? Why or why not?

5. When will you plan to fast from engaging in digital spaces? What preemptive ways will you plan to protect your vulnerabilities?

6. The author makes the case that since we are clearly digitally expectant, we should be spiritually expectant. Along with his

suggestions for this, what other ways could you foster spiritual expectancy?

7. As you break the fast, what compulsions have you identified? What do they tell you?

CHAPTER 5

Cultivate a Transformed Heart

IN THE LAST CHAPTER, we learned that a spiritually disciplined life requires consistently offering our attention to God, others, and the world. As these digital distractions often steal such precious attention, now we address our hearts, which always guide our attention. Distractions are often the excuse for why we struggle to follow Christ: I don't have enough time. I'm stressed. I need a break. The truth is that distractions can mask the deeper reason we don't give God our attention: because we don't *want* to. We'd rather be comforted than changed, and discipline sounds difficult. We'd rather give our attention to digital spaces—or a whole host of other things—instead of God simply because, if we're honest, we love those things. So if the things we love ultimately guide our attention, how do we make *God* the One we love? We cultivate our hearts to value God's character and good design, letting right desire pull us forward. Enough duty, we need God's beauty to transform what and how we love!

Because we are whole people (mind, desires, will, and a physical body), training the heart requires actively developing our mind, desires, and will for the renewal of the *whole self*.[1] We live in a world that prizes self-discovery, but true knowledge of self is dependent on knowledge of God, which is not intuitive, and the process of learning is never complete.[2] We know who we are in light of who He is, not who we define ourselves (or Him) to be.[3] As we've explored in previous chapters, if we don't learn firsthand what He says about Himself, then we create a god in our own image based on our interpretations of other people. By consistently reading God's Word, the Spirit enables clearer sight through God's own self-revelation in the text and, ultimately, in Jesus Christ. When we apply this knowledge of God's character and wisdom to life, it is called sound Christian doctrine, which is a primary aid to life in God's wisdom.[4]

Where God's wisdom leads to right desires, right desires motivate discipline to surrender all of life to God's good design. Untrained hearts miss the design under the desire and compulsively feed desire outside of God's design. We fill loneliness with pornography, insecurity with dependence, a failing marriage with idolizing children, or overperforming at work to avoid pain at home. This forms an identity out of seeking to cope rather than receiving our identity by seeking God's wisdom in His Word and among His people.

As those committed to becoming healthier Christians, we pursue discipline in giving our attention to the right things, but to do that, we must *want* the right things. To want the right things, we need a transformed heart. So, how do we get a transformed heart? *We read God's Word, we read God's family, we commit to learning, and we rehearse reality.*

READ GOD'S WORD

With three small children, many days Carly and I are running together side by side in the thick of life. We can focus so tightly on daily schedules that we fail to turn face-to-face and simply be present with each other. After the last kid is asleep and the house is reset, it's lights out. It's easy to let the hurry of life distract from facing each other, listening, and caring for each other. We've learned that a healthy life and marriage require us to run side by side, yes, but also to stop and gaze, face-to-face.[5]

Many Christians expect time in the Scriptures to be unhindered face-to-face conversation with God, audible direction, and soul-stirring worship, leaving us radiating glory while walking down the mountain.

For those of us who lack shining faces *again*, we wonder if anyone is at our side. We hoped for something: an answer to trouble, help with a decision, some measure of peace. This tempts us to ask the text (and the divine Author) to answer *our* questions instead of listening to the questions the Bible is answering.[6] It's a natural, albeit misguided approach. We are looking for the wrong thing and frazzled because we overexpect something deceptively simple: spending time with God in His Word over the course of our lives.

The Christian life necessitates side-by-side and face-to-face interaction with God's Word throughout all of life. While I have an annual reading plan, I also need time in the Word with no goal except of delighting in God. The constant side-by-side presence of God through His Word and turning face-to-face for unhurried delight renews our hearts.

If you quietly panic when someone assumes you know a Bible character, or only think of Indiana Jones when asked about the ark of the covenant, you're not alone. Many of us think we know the Bible better than we do, and while you might believe familiarity breeds contempt, in this case familiarity breeds unsuspecting unfamiliarity.[7]

Commentaries and sermons are helpful aids to learning the Bible, but there is no substitute for firsthand knowledge. If you read a confusing passage and jump to let someone else explain it, slow down. Treating time in the Scriptures as a fact-finding mission instead of sacred space with God can lead us to disappear into someone else's conclusions instead of taking the time to find our own. The only way we learn firsthand is by reading for ourselves.

Here are some ways to practice the discipline of reading God's Word.

1. Read the whole Bible throughout your whole life.

This might seem basic: find a reading plan and stick with it. If you miss a day(s), pick back up and keep going. Pursue incremental growth instead of overnight perfection. Pick a plan and get going, no need to wait for January to roll around.

Only through consistent reading will our interpretation of life be confronted with God's own self-revelation, His design of the world, and the story of true life with Him. To merely read the Bible when we feel like it is to treat God's Word like a vaccine instead of our lifeline to reality.

Running side-by-side through regular reading produces the gifts of perspective and repetition—not to mention the increasingly rare ability to offer long and deep spans of attention to something meaningful. Now let's look at a type of face-to-face spiritual discipline.

2. Read God's Word slowly for delight.

Throughout history God's people have used different disciplines to read God's Word well. One way Christians have done this is through this simple progression: read, reflect, respond, and rest.[8] Below is an example of the discipline with a beloved passage: the upper room discourse in John 14–17.

READ: I read through this longer passage until something makes me pause: either a thought, phrase, or something I hadn't noticed before. I'll read the verses several times out loud, usually writing it down in my journal by hand.

REFLECT: Thinking upon the scene in Scripture, I place myself in the moment by imagining details like I'm watching in real time (especially fruitful with Gospel narratives). In reading John, I picture the disciples and Jesus around the dinner table, hearing things are about to change.

RESPOND: Sitting with the text longer than I do on a normal day, these spaces allow room for being attentive to what God might say through what I have read or heard. I pray especially around the parts of the passage that jumped out at me, trusting that the Spirit is working to convict me in some way or opening my eyes to a truth I have overlooked in times past.

REST: Listening for God through the text, I work to keep my thoughts quiet. I sometimes pray or sing a lyric that comes to mind. I'll ask God if I need to do anything today in response to what I've read.

This practice of face-to-face reading trains me to be less concerned with checking a box than I am with quieting my soul. Side-by-side or face-to-face, we need to read God's Word alone and with others.

3. Listen to the public reading of Scripture.

Over the last few years, a growing community of friends gather once a month. They grab dinner, sit together, and open their Bibles.

Seems familiar, right? Here's the twist: they take turns reading through a book of the Bible out loud. Slowly and steadily, they sit under God's spoken Word. No sermons, no commentary, just the Scriptures. If you think about it, most of these New Testament letters were first read aloud with others, and we mostly read them in silence by ourselves. Paul tells Timothy to "devote [himself] to the public reading of Scripture" (1 Tim. 4:13 ESV), and we do well to heed Paul's advice. When we practice the discipline of the public reading of Scripture, we notice things we skip over when we quietly read them on our own. The text breathes on us, and as we gather together, we expect to hear God speak.

Gather some friends and read the text aloud an hour at a time. Again, the goal is faithful endurance, not speed. May God meet you in the public reading of His Word!

READ GOD'S FAMILY

To cultivate a transformed heart, we first read God's Word, but we don't stop there. Next, our heart is enlivened as we read

God's family across the ages. We read of how saints lived faithfully in changing times and consider the ways God's Word has been applied across the generations. This helps us value voices of the past and what they can bring to our present.

In addressing the value of reading older books, C. S. Lewis describes how modern books are often speaking to older arguments, and without a knowledge of the preceding conversation we might be swayed while only possessing a portion of the facts. He says:

> [A new book] has to be tested against the great body of Christian thought down the ages, and all its hidden implications (often unsuspected by the author himself) have to be brought to light. Often it cannot be fully understood without the knowledge of a good many other modern books. If you join at eleven o'clock a conversation which began at eight you will often not see the real bearing of what is said. Remarks which seem to you very ordinary will produce laughter or irritation and you will not see why—the reason, of course, being that the earlier stages of the conversation have given them a special point. In the same way sentences in a modern book which look quite ordinary

> may be directed at some other book; in this way you may be led to accept what you would have indignantly rejected if you knew its real significance.[9]

We need perspective that runs centuries deep, not decades. Christianity has this in spades if we know where to look.

Practicing this discipline is simple: choose a historical Christian figure and study their work. Everyone should have a mentor or three from the past. We want to read works that have stood the test of time. In the appendices is a short list of suggestions to get started. I find setting reasonable page-count goals helps to start small and build steam as you go.

How do you read? By interacting with their thoughts and asking yourself: Where do you agree with them? Where do they frustrate or confuse you? What is unique to their thoughts about God and the Christian life? If you read with friends, it will sharpen your thinking and challenge you to keep moving through a text, even when it's difficult.

There are treasures to be found in the works of God's family. As with the Bible, "raking is easy, you get leaves. Digging is hard, but you may get diamonds."[10] Let's dig with God's family, for when we see what He has done across the ages, our hearts can't help but be lit aflame in worship and adoration of Him.

COMMIT TO LEARNING

One night at the end of a class I was teaching at our church, a woman in her sixties approached me and said: "I've been in church forty years, and no one has ever told me this. I think of all I could have done differently if I knew Him this way. I had no idea that is what the Scriptures were talking about." As we learned in chapter 3, you can't discover these "old truths recently forgotten"[11] without committing yourself to learning. Having a *sense* that you should read God's Word and God's family doesn't mean you're actually doing it. Nor does reading a book about these things or posting online about conversations that have to do with them. You have to commit to learn and actually follow through. What helps here is to remember that actively engaging in the life of the mind is not a merely academic pursuit, or a way to level up your smarts; rather, it is a way to transform your heart and grow your love for God. As Jen Wilkin says, "The heart cannot love what the mind does not know."[12] In other words, learn with all attentiveness of mind so that you might love with all depth of heart.

If we resist the call to become a lifelong learner, we will naturally allow culture's love of ease to shape our view of the Christian life. We will treat our life with God flippantly, and we will not grow healthier. We will expect growth in Christ to happen passively, to be anything but costly, and to require anything but work from us. But if we choose to learn and follow through with the spiritual disciplines that help us develop the life of our mind, though they be costly, we will find that they have trained us for godliness, which Scripture says is "of value in every way, as it holds promise for the present life and also for the life to come" (1 Tim. 4:8 ESV).

Here are two recommended disciplines that will help you commit to learning:

1. Join a class, book club, or discussion group.

Learning about God thrives in conversation within community. Learning with others helps form our thoughts while growing our competency and confidence about the things of God. We study, reflect, and take time to articulate what we're learning by figuring out how to say it in our own words.

Entering a learning environment can be intimidating. Who wants to go first and get the answer wrong? Even worse is when we're talking about God because *nobody* wants to get God wrong. What would happen?

Well, you wouldn't combust. God is big enough for you to be in process. We will always be beginners in the things of God, and so there is much grace for wherever you start, but you must start!

2. Share what you're learning with others.

Discipling others is a key safeguard against the mind turning inward to prize knowledge over love. Paul said as much to the Corinthians: "Knowledge puffs up, but love builds up. If anyone thinks he knows anything, he does not yet know it as he ought to know it. But if anyone loves God, he is known by him" (1 Cor. 8:1–3).

Knowledge cannot terminate on ourselves. All gifts are ultimately intended for use to build up the church. We are "fellow citizens with the saints, and members of God's household, built on the foundation of the apostles and prophets, with Christ Jesus himself as the cornerstone. In him the whole building, being put together, grows into a holy temple in the Lord" (Eph. 2:19–21). The Christian life is about life together in God, the people of God grown and built together as the dwelling place of God on earth. No one is asking you to be an expert, but you do need to be present, willing to listen, share, and speak truth.

If you have children, spend time teaching them God's Word in ways they can understand. Look for teachable moments in daily life, pointing out God's character, design, and beauty to them in ways that are *normal and invitational.* Sow seeds always; reap when able.

If you have coworkers or friends who are interested in Jesus, invite them to study a Gospel narrative with you. Talk about what you see together, and cultivate questions rather than dispense answers while you pray for God to work.

If you're a small-group leader, volunteer, supervisor, teacher, or employee, pray for a space to share the beauty of Christ. Then look for God to provide opportunities to join in what He's doing.

REHEARSE REALITY

Of all the moments requiring my attention during the week, the Lord's Supper is one of my favorites. We focus on the person and work of Christ while sitting with the family of God, and it reminds me who I really am: loved by Christ, reconciled to God, indwelt by the Spirit, and part of a larger story and a family of faith. It helps me rehearse the certainty of my future hope and anchors me in reality.

The church serves to form and maintain our identities in Christ individually **and** communally.[13] Western individualism trains us to think our choices simply affect ourselves, while in truth the body of Christ is an interdependent community, and we have a vested interest when it comes to maturing in Christ. We need one another, and we need to rehearse truth while *physically together* as often as we can.

We commonly think about giving our attention to *receive* something. Rehearsing reality puts our attention to work *producing* something: recalling and proclaiming God's reality. Where we use our attention to rehearse reality, we build confidence in future grace based on God's past faithfulness.

Here are three disciplines to help you rehearse reality:

1. Gather locally and regularly with the people of God.

"Let us hold on to the confession of our hope without wavering, since he who promised is faithful. And let us consider one another in order to provoke love and good works, not neglecting to gather together, as some are in the habit of doing, but encouraging each other, and all the more as you see the day approaching" (Heb. 10:23–25).

Being physically together matters. Witnessing baptisms and hearing testimonies of God's saving grace rehearses and strengthens our hope in Christ. It reminds us of who we were and who God is making us into.

If you're not already, join and worship at a local church. Show up for a lifetime of Sundays and let the Spirit transform your heart through the Word sung, preached, and proclaimed in baptism and the Lord's Supper. Christian, your primary identity is that of a child of God and, by extension, a brother or sister to many others. You can't become this on your own, for learning your place requires your presence in the household alongside your other siblings. We need one another as the body of Christ.

2. Share what God has done.

There was a time in my life when I was overcome by anxiety and did not know how to find peace. I was a Christian but feared God was not as good as He says He is, and that what He said about me wasn't true. But then God helped me trust and delight in Christ. Since then I have found freedom from fear and live with peace. Do you have a story like that?[14]

These five sentences are a simple way to share the truth of Jesus with others through life experiences. Most of us know we should share our faith but wrestle with guilt if we don't risk awkwardness or rejection to speak of Jesus.

Sharing your faith is not an all-or-nothing endeavor. Loving your neighbors is stronger than pulling a bait-and-switch conversation tactic. No one gets tricked into loving Christ; they respond by seeing His beauty. We love people because they are made in the image of God, and we live with consistency that images the true, good, and the beautiful nature of God. We actively share about Jesus, and we love as we have been loved.

Sharing what Christ has done is the fruit of our attention being surrendered to God and shaped by the Spirit. We not only do what we know we should; we *want* to do it because our loves are guiding our actions.

3. Sing to God alongside others and by yourself.

Corporate singing is something various cultures throughout history have done in all sorts of contexts to remember stories or build connection through joining together; but American culture today doesn't have much space for this practice. Apart from concerts, or maybe singing the national anthem at a baseball game (and even then, you're more likely to hear a soloist perform it than sing it yourself alongside your fellow attendees), the Sunday service at church is one of the only times lots of people sing common songs together.

Songs are a powerful way to pass down the faith, for they remind us of the story of God and what He's done in the world. They remind us of what's true when we're forgetful. They instill confidence in us when we're scared. They speak comfort over us when we're weary. They tell us the true story of Christianity when we've gotten swept up in countless other false narratives. They also are offered to God Himself as a means of worship and encouragement to our family in Christ. There are days my heart is weary, and I need to hear the songs of faith sung loud. Where my faith is tired or weak, the faith of another can lift my head in song. Singing aloud among the saints changes your perspective and strengthens your faith in God like nothing else can!

How often do you sing to God? I encourage you to sing to Him on Sundays, of course, alongside your fellow church members. But I also encourage you to sing to Him while you're alone, throughout the week, in moments you need to remember what's true. In just a few short minutes, you'll not only offer your attention and heart to Christ, but in return, you'll be reminded anew of God's reality.

DISCUSSION QUESTIONS

1. The author makes the case that your attention and your heart are connected. How have you found this to be true?

2. One way to transform your heart is through reading God's Word and God's family. When it comes to your Bible reading time, what does this discipline currently look like in your daily life? How would you like to see it change in the following weeks and months? When it comes to reading God's family, how might this practice transform your heart and attention span?

3. Why must we commit to learning? In what ways does the life of the mind affect the depth of our heart?

4. Summarize what it means to rehearse reality. How do you see your local church doing this? In what ways might you grow in this discipline?

5. Why is being part of a physically gathered community so important (whether that's the church or other gathered experiences)? If you feel internal resistance toward offering your physical presence in church (or in other areas of life), explore that. Why do you think you feel this way?

6. How might you seek to be more present with others? Consider ways you might be present for those who might be sick or elderly and who don't have anyone else. Also consider opportunities like dinner parties, coffee dates, and other normal, everyday interactions.

7. What would your five-sentence testimony be? Remember, the goal is presence and right action that flows from a right heart, not simply the right words. You can't save anyone, but the One you serve can!

CHAPTER 6

Learn to Listen

I OFTEN FEEL LIKE it's way too noisy in my head. Deadlines, tasks, unchecked boxes, and plans all swirl together as I try to be present and productive in my home and at work. In all the noise, I feel hurried inside. In this state I can't hear God clearly. Even if I sat still, often my mind hasn't stopped moving. Can you relate?

A pastor in California once asked his mentor: "What do I need to do in order to grow in my walk with Christ?"

His mentor, Dallas Willard, responded to him: "You must ruthlessly eliminate hurry from your life. Hurry is the great enemy of the spiritual life."[1]

Talk about a phrase that will haunt you. When we can't process our emotions and get flooded by them, we can't think. When we run from our inner world to the safety of the digital one, we avoid thinking. When we leave our hearts untrained, we trade thinking for desire. Because attention has been hurried into pieces, many of us lack the capacity to listen to the right things at the right time with the right focus.

In order to hear the Holy Spirit, we must listen to what is happening inside and around us. We listen in prayer and by reading the Scriptures.

Jesus tells a parable about four kinds of seed being scattered on the ground. Three of the four hit the dirt and fail to flourish. I'm interested in the fourth seed that "fell on good ground and it grew up, producing fruit that increased thirty, sixty, and a hundred times" (Mark 4:8).

Jesus opens the parable by saying, "Listen!," and then He finishes by adding, "Let anyone who has ears to hear listen" (vv. 3, 9). It's said that this parable points to receiving the truth about the kingdom of God, that to be a disciple of the kingdom means hearing and remaining focused on the message of the kingdom in such a way that one is defined by it. The key to spiritual formation is the willingness to listen, the practice of the discipline of listening, and responding appropriately to the received word.[2]

How can I receive the word if I can't sit still enough to listen? How can I become the kind of person who hears clearly and responds quickly to God's voice in my life? What message am I sending to others if I say I love God but my actions show I treasure hurry? How can I really see or listen to them?

The discipline of listening helps us attend to God, ourselves, and others as we steward our time and attention.

The parable points us to become the kind of person who is able to hear and respond to God's invitation to life. As Klyne Snodgrass would say, it's the kind of "hearing that leads to productive living."[3]

So, how does a person begin the process of learning how to listen? Especially in a culture that trains us to be impulsive, frenzied, scattered, and quick-tongued? How does this aspect of offering our attentiveness get cultivated?

Here are some ideas for disciplining yourself in this area.

SIT STILL

There are a few ways to develop the ability to listen, but one of prerequisites to any of them is learning to sit still. This can mean in body and in mind, or it can mean either/or. (For example, plenty of people can go for a jog but enjoy a stilled mind while doing so. On the other hand, plenty of people need to have a still body *and* a still mind in order to truly hear anything.) The point is that if you are still in the way you need to be, you have a way better shot at hearing something than if you're frenzied.

For me, it looks like making the time to be the first one up in our house. I sit in silence (and the dark) with my booklight, thinking about the day ahead. I pray over my calendar, talking with God about each meeting or task. I consider my family and what they will face that day. I read from the Word and write down thoughts or prayers in response.

Then I try to sit and listen to God. When a thought comes into view, I consider it, write it down if needed, and return to listening. Often God brings a person to mind, and I make a note to text or call them later in the day. If I know of something going on with them, I pray for them. I sit still and take deep breaths. I look at the trees in the backyard. I thank God for His kindness. Unhurried silence makes space for listening.

The more decades that pass, the more I crave time to sit and listen. It sets the tone for my day. I acknowledge I've woken up into a day where God is already at work, and He's inviting me to head into the office with Him. This is a sharp contrast to the mornings I sleep in, get distracted, or fail to settle my heart before the hurry knocks. Life feels loud in those moments.

What might stillness look like for you? If you make space for it, I guarantee you'll not only get better at listening; you'll get better at offering the whole category of your attention to God over the long haul of your life.

BE A FRIEND WHO LISTENS

There is a kind of listening where you feel not just heard but *seen* by the other. I hope you've experienced this from a trusted friend. It is a ministry in itself as it communicates presence, attention, and care—all of which serve to heal the wounds caused by our world. True listening is a willingness to meet our friends in their pain and sit with them, despite our inability to fix it. This kind of listening comes from a settled heart.

We live in rhythms of processing our emotions, coming to terms with our noisy hearts, and quieting our needy selves before our Maker. We can sit with pain, disappointment, confusion, and need with no compulsion to wash our hands when we leave. When we have been comforted by God, we can comfort others (2 Cor. 1). Because there are things only Jesus can fix, we use discernment to leave space for Him to work what we can't.[4] We remain present and attentive to the person in front of us, offering a nonanxious presence borne from time with God in our own lives.

Next time you're with a loved one, try your hand at being a friend that doesn't just catch up, but *listens* with the aim for the other person to feel truly seen and heard. This practice will not only teach you how to slow down; it will make you more like Christ over time, who as we know, fully sees and compassionately hears us when we come to Him as our most trusted friend.

LIVE SIMPLY

The writer of Hebrews tells us, "Be satisfied [content] with what you have, for he himself has said, 'I will never leave you or abandon you'" (Heb. 13:5). Right before that He says, "Keep your life free from the love of money." I wouldn't come right out and say I love money, but I often spend like it can provide all my needs.

Who you have—meaning, Christ—will outlast what you can buy. "Be satisfied [content] with what you have, for he himself has said, 'I will never leave you or abandon you.'" When you have less to keep track of, you have more margin to be present to what matters—more time to listen. With compassion, Jesus told the rich young ruler that his attachment to earthly treasure was the problem (Mark 10). In the Sermon on the Mount, Jesus advises that the things we store up here can be stolen and destroyed (or sold in an estate sale), and it's better to store up treasure in heaven because our heart follows what we love (Matt. 6:19–21).

Living simply means determining what is most central to life and then removing the noise that distracts us. It's the obligations, activities, events, options, and desire for significance that keeps things hurried. When we create space in life, we can sit still and listen. We can train our attentiveness. When our compulsion is to acquire instead of abide, it is a warning sign to change some things.

LIVE SLOWLY

If I'm not paying attention, I will run at a speed faster than the pace of presence I ultimately want. A few years ago, I was hurrying between meetings across cities and handling some issues with work and extended family. I felt like I was juggling while handcuffed to a treadmill set on high speed.

Then within the span of two weeks, I got three speeding tickets.

I slowed down *real* quick.

Maybe you've also discovered cruise control this way. The defensive driving course only served to highlight the stress and adrenaline I'd been running on for weeks. Ultimately, I was thankful for being pulled over as it forced slowness when I wouldn't. In the years since, I've come to see the anxiety of hurry as flashing lights warning that life is moving too fast. One author calls it "learning to live at the pace of grace."[5]

Life is not a race. Try living slowly. When we live slowly and simply with stillness and compassion for others, we are most postured not just to give God our attention but also to hear from Him in return.

DISCUSSION QUESTIONS

1. Do you feel like you're living life in a hurry? Where do you think that comes from?

2. Why is it nearly impossible to grow in our spiritual lives if we don't have the ability to listen?

3. What helps you sit still? What obstacles prevent you from sitting still? What steps could you take to minimize the obstacles?

4. What does it look like practically to listen to God? Consider scheduling time to listen in prayer instead of launching into a list of requests or needs, asking God what He wants you to hear and being silent before Him.

5. What keeps you from holding space for others? How might you pursue emotional health and maturity for yourself so that you may be able to sit with others in their pain? *Note:* The underlying discipline here is to care for others like you would hope they care for you. This takes practice, self-denial, and a listening heart.

6. What could living simply look like for you? In what areas of life do you need to work to create margin, whether that be in mental, spiritual, or financial spheres? Where do you need to do less?

7. Consider the last few chapters on attention. What practices might you begin today to develop more discipline around your incredibly valuable attention? Consider going for a walk without an intention of tracking steps or a checklist of items to mentally work through. Between meetings or locations, take a few moments to slow down and spend time praying.

DIMENSION TWO

Disciplining Our Emotions

I Go among Trees

Wendell Berry

I go among trees and sit still.
All my stirring becomes quiet
around me like circles on water.
My tasks lie in their places
where I left them, asleep like cattle.

Then what is afraid of me comes
and lives a while in my sight.
What it fears in me leaves me,
and the fear of me leaves it.
It sings, and I hear its song.

Then what I am afraid of comes.
I live for a while in its sight.

What I fear in it leaves it,
and the fear of it leaves me.
It sings, and I hear its song.

After days of labor,
mute in my consternations,
I hear my song at last,
and I sing it. As we sing,
the day turns, the trees move.[1]

CHAPTER 7

Process Your Emotions

WE'VE COVERED WHY OUR attention is important to offer up to God in intentional ways, and that's part of a spiritually disciplined life that people tend to naturally nod along with. We know we should give our attention less to our digital life and more toward the Scriptures and prayer, yet we struggle with the right desire to actually do the things we know are best for us. To become a healthy Christian, we must offer *all* of ourselves to God, not merely our attention, as important as that is. Our emotional life must also be offered to God in disciplined ways, for God wants every part of us. Our head *and* our heart.

So, how does one become more spiritually disciplined in the area of emotions? In this section, we'll consider two ways: *processing our emotions* and *trusting God with every emotion.*

One of my regular disciplines is to chase quiet. I load up my kayak, hop in a local lake, and paddle away from currents and screens.

I drop anchor and wait for the waves inside to match the calm outside.

Recently on the water I read "I Go among Trees" by Wendell Berry, as seen on pages 106–7, reminding myself of just how important it is to quiet my own soul and take inventory of my own thoughts and emotions, hard as that may be.

Do you ever try to avoid your emotions? Me too.

Most of us aren't sure what to do with all we feel, so we avoid sitting still among the trees of our life. We distract ourselves to escape being alone because we are terrified of, ashamed, or disappointed by who we might have to face when we stop moving: ourselves.

We are complex, embodied creatures, and emotions are tricky business. What we feel and think are gifts from God to know Him, ourselves, and others rightly. Learning how to process emotions is an essential part of Christian maturity; however, they don't come with an instruction manual in the glove box of our souls. If left unprocessed, emotions reinforce disordered desires and distort interpretations of our own experience. Surrendering and discipling how we handle our emotions enables us to move through them toward productive action in life with God.

PROCESS YOUR EMOTIONS

Over the years, a few colleagues have walked into my office, shut the door, and said four specific words that drop my stomach in a heartbeat: *we need to talk.*

From that moment I'm in prime fight-or-flight mode, readying to defend myself. My brain is on alert, and if I'm not careful, my heart rate clogs my ears from hearing what we *need* to talk about.

Whatever the issue is, and however good my relationship is with the person who walked in my office, with those four words memories show up in my body with their baggage in hand. In these moments, it seems impossible to regulate my emotions.

Have you ever felt like that—like your emotions were in the driver's seat?

Emotions (how our body responds to events) and our feelings (how we interpret those responses) are the normal ways we interact with the world around us.[1] These reactions and interpretations are impacted by sin in us, sin we commit, and sin committed against us. If you've ever assumed the worst of someone, you've had a reaction impacted by sin. Cut off in traffic? *That* guy. Selfish.

Then there are times you have a *spirited* discussion with someone you love. There are words like *always* and *never* lying scattered on the ground, and you step on land mines, saying things you don't believe just to keep it even. Your brain is flooded with adrenaline, heart rate is up, mouth tastes like metal, and breath is shallow. Your ability to think critically has been sidelined for the rest of the game.

I once heard a human resource specialist talk about this sidelining of critical thinking. With the front of your brain flooded, it needs a reset, which takes two full minutes to flush out. To provide the necessary break, she suggested actively engaging your critical thinking—with math. It's hard to be offended while doing long division.

The two-minute time-out is one way to handle your emotions because it signals you're no longer in control and interrupts your brain's interpretation of your bodily experience. It's good to recognize emotions, name them, and then move through to productive action. This way you regain the driver's seat.

At a minimum, we need to be aware that we have more feelings than happy and angry. Below is a tool often used to help individuals name what they are feeling, as naming an emotion is key to healthy processing. Feelings can easily mask themselves as something else. Insecurity might feel like being hesitant, and confidence might feel aggressive depending on how you respond to the moment.

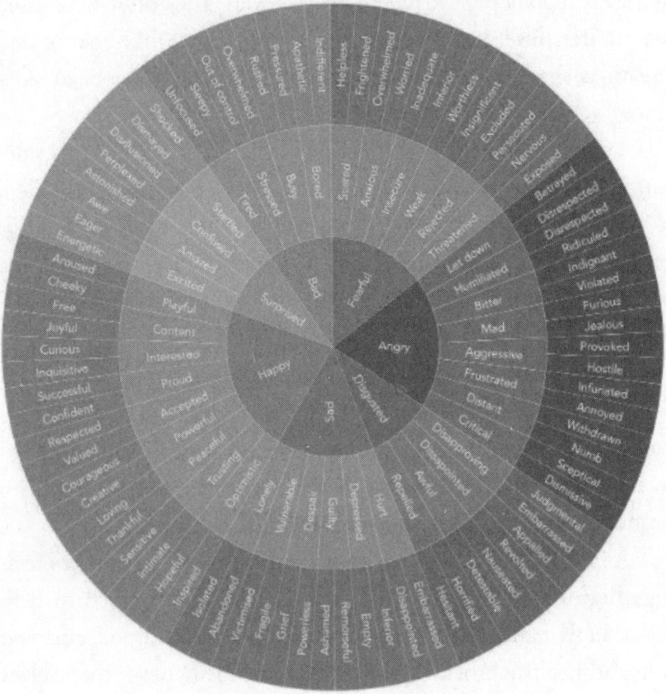

The Feelings Wheel[2]

Save a wheel like this on your phone. When you feel a strong emotion, chase it down to the outer ring, name it, and explore why you're feeling that way. Growing in awareness of your feelings and what you tell yourself about them is important.

Knowing what makes you angry, triggers shame, or catapults you out of the driver's seat not only helps uproot the lies in your heart, it makes space for you to then move toward God's way of living instead.

In the end, disciplining yourself to process your emotions helps you understand how your feelings are affecting not only you as God's vessel but others around you, too—which, in turn, will help you better obey the Great Commandment of loving God and others.

For some other ideas on disciplining yourself to process your emotions, consider these.

1. Pay attention, pray, and get curious.

Our bodies pick up on things physically long before we do cognitively. When you get that sinking feeling, it's the same chemical in your brain and gut saying, *Hey, something's not right.*

I know this one well. Anxiety is the unwanted companion I've had most of my life. When I begin to worry, I instinctively breathe shallowly, lowering oxygen to my body. My ability to react rationally fades as the loop of brain chemicals, thoughts, and reactions play scripts of interpretations I've built over the years.

In these moments, I encourage you to practice the discipline of paying attention to what your body is telling you. It's hard, I know. You just want to push past things and not address them. But stop and take inventory of what your body is doing, and then direct whatever you discover toward God.

For me, it looks like focusing on grounding my mind in my body and not my thoughts. I sit up straight in a chair, drop my shoulders, breathe deeply, and wiggle my toes. I find a way to stop overfunctioning and give my body what it needs to hear God's truth clearly in prayer. I ask for help from God and even others to consider the source of anxiety, holding it to get a good look at what is true, what is accusation, attack, or a wrong interpretation of events. I let the worst-case scenario play out in my mind and rehearse that even if it happened, God would still be good. As I hold the feeling in prayer, I remind myself I am feeling this emotion, but I am not my feelings. As many have said, our feelings are real, but they're not reliable. They change quickly and are impacted by a host of factors like diet, body chemistry, sleep, and exercise. Knowing God is committed to me, I make peace with being a work in process and move through the moment.

Maybe your anxiety is driven by the visions of perfection you see on social media, your friends on their fourth vacation of the year, or the fear of being the one friend not invited to the party. Our hearts are tossed into a bouncy castle of coveting, consumerism, comparison, discontent, dopamine, and cortisol.

While processing your emotions, try to exercise curiosity instead of shame. Often we scold ourselves for being impacted by things that are simply a normal part of being human. Instead of despising your humanity, look for what triggered the reaction and treat yourself with compassion, breathe deeply, and rehearse God's reality. We are all works in progress. When you discipline yourself to pay attention to what your body is telling you about your heart and treat your emotional responses with curiosity, you are becoming not just a healthier Christian but a healthier human being all around. (Not to mention, the watching lost world will find you attractive, for you'll be one of those rare people who seems emotionally in tune but, at the same time, does not fly by the seat of their emotions.)

2. Schedule daily breaks to process in prayer.

Maintaining presence with God throughout the day can be difficult. To help with this, I use hinges in my day for prayerful conversation with God to process what's happened, how I'm feeling, and what is next on the schedule. It's a historical discipline called *praying the hours* and is easily one of the most accessible spiritual disciplines I've come across for pausing to be present to God. I have adapted a version I first learned from Zack Eswine in his work, *The Imperfect Pastor*.[3]

As a method to create space to process our emotions with God, we take the day as it comes in four blocks:

Morning (6 a.m.–12 p.m.)

Afternoon (12 p.m.–6 p.m.)

Evening (6 p.m.–10 p.m.)

Night (10 p.m.–6 a.m.)

At the close of each portion of the day, I take five to ten minutes to recognize and confess temptations I faced, sins I committed, and emotions I'm feeling or breezed past. I think about the email that's bothering me, and I ask for grace to assume the best of others. I trust God to be enough in handling my failures and needs. I preach the gospel to myself, that I am being made new and am loved by my Creator. I thank God for specific things, and then I stop talking altogether. I listen and breathe deeply as I sit in God's presence. When it's time to move on, I look at the coming portion of the day and ask for grace for the conversations to be had, people to care for, and work to be done.

Try scheduling these hinges into your day and see what happens. Prayer is a two-way conversation. Make sure to listen. The Spirit is moving; most of us just need to sit still a bit longer.

3. Revisit your own story.

It's no secret in our house that the movie *About Time* wreaks havoc on my emotions. It's not that time travel tugs at my heart-strings, but its many themes touch on different seasons of my own life. Chief among these is the fear that I'll miss a moment with the person in front of me. With all I've got, I want to be present with the people in my life and the moments we share: the mundane, the beautiful, and the hard. This kind of presence requires us to first be present to our own story. If we leave the interpretation of life we've written along the way in an unprocessed state, we can't hold space to rejoice or mourn with those around us.

The discipline of charting our stories with God is a fruitful way to be present to all the major turning points of our lives.[4] This allows us to process our stories, looking at the moments (good, bad, and ugly) that have significantly impacted our direction. Our narrative of life shapes who we have and will become, which means it's important to reinterpret our story with God throughout life. Our memories of the past shape how we respond to the present. If left alone, they will shape our future with increasingly stronger influence. Snodgrass reminds us that [personal] "histories are to be remembered and processed for truth and learning, not lived in or given ultimate defining force. What a person gives ultimate defining force is the key identity question, and for Christians, only Christ is given ultimate defining force."[5]

In the appendices I've included a worksheet from The Paterson Center for processing the turning points of your life (used with permission). A turning point is a decision, event, person, episode, or experience that significantly turned the direction of your life (for good or ill). One way to identify turning points is to ask: "How did this turn change how I think, work, engage, relate to God and others, and lead me to this point in my life?"[6]

We're meant to be present in our lives, not withdrawing to avoid pain. Find movement toward health by revisiting your story and letting God help reinterpret what you narrated along the way. Let Christ alone be the defining force of your history and identity.

4. Find a Christian conversation partner.

Growing as a Christian—moving forward toward the sanctified future self we're meant to be—requires us to work out our feelings instead of ignoring (or stuffing down) the emotional component that God Himself intentionally built into the human experience, and often the most profitable way to work them out is with a trusted conversation partner. Christians are the sole group invited and equipped to receive one another with the grace and comfort we have received from Christ (2 Cor. 1:4). We use discernment and trust certain friends to receive us with (imperfect but effortful) grace, which images God to one another in the Christian life. No one likes feeling vulnerable, waiting on the edge of our seats for the moment of truth, wondering: *Will this person accept or abandon me?* When someone pulls back in that moment, we feel shame that not only the action we've confessed is wrong but *we* are wrong.

If you have been met by the love of Christ, who knows the worst about you (even the future stuff you don't know yet), then you know He does not shame or reject you. He takes your shame. Yes, you have done terrible things. Yes, He will help you experience change where change is needed; *and* yes, you are loved. Living into this truth as those Christ renews into His image enables us to hold space for others to share their stories. We listen, receive, and image the grace of God by connecting with them in a moment ripe for shame.[7] We can't transform their hearts, but as we focus on embodying God's love to others, we can ask that He do the work we can't, reinterpreting their stories in light of His heart for them.

An example of this from my life is that Tuesday nights after my kids are in bed, I meet up with my conversation partners. We confess what's not working for us in daily life, where we have sinned, and where we need help. We've committed to share and pray for one another, together. We encourage, interact with, and counsel one another. Then I walk back home. That's it.

One of the guys recently moved back from Nashville, and he brought the form of this discipline of confession from his time at Immanuel Church. Sam Allberry, one of the pastors at Immanuel, calls this Walking in the Light and describes it in an article entitled "I Trust Them with My Sins." Sam brings two passages to bear on this discipline:[8]

> Therefore, confess your sins to one another and pray for one another, so that you may be healed. The prayer of a righteous person is very powerful in its effect. (James 5:16)

Which leads to the fruit of 1 John 1:7:

> If we walk in the light as he himself is in the light, we have fellowship with one another, and the blood of Jesus his Son cleanses us from all sin.

It might seem small, but the clarity of this time has been a welcome opportunity for us to minister to one another within Christian friendship. Most weeks I look forward to our time; other times I feel the itch to skip. Since it's a time of confession, it makes sense that fear, shame, or schedule might all provide reasons to stay home. The discipline of showing up reinforces that grace is real and I need the family of God.

Identify friends you can *trust with your sins*, as Sam would say. This doesn't mean you trust them to cover up your sins in the shadows. It means you walk in the light with one another about what's really going in your lives and fight together in prayer.

Each of us needs someone else to see the things we don't want anyone to know, and we need them to receive us like Christ does: acknowledging the weight and consequence of our actions, while also letting us realize we are known, kept, and loved.[9] The reality is, not just anyone can be this person for you. If you have a person you can trust, someone who will model Christ's grace to you, cultivate that conversation with purpose. If you don't have someone like this in your life, I recommend you find a Christian who is a licensed counselor that you trust. Either ask a local church or a wise friend for a recommendation. Many churches have care ministries that hold leader-facilitated groups for this precise reason: to speak your shame out loud, find that you're not alone, turn down the path of wisdom where you need to, and be met with the transforming love of Christ.

Christian, we can only love as we've been loved. Jesus has seen our worst and isn't going anywhere. Receive others the way Christ receives you, and model love that covers shame. Life is hard, emotions are complex, and we need to make sure we are interpreting things rightly.

A few notes: I want to acknowledge there are times when our stories contain abuse, trauma, or neglect. We are impacted by our own sin or sin done to us. If this is your experience, you may be well served by meeting with a Christian who specializes in caring for these circumstances as you engage healing.

There are times when your friends are not the sounding board you need, and that's normal. Processing through life with a trained counselor can be as healthy as an annual physical. Many counselors I know treat clients over four to six sessions instead of ongoing appointments. The goal is to find movement through the issue at hand, equip the client with tools to process and interpret rightly, and then be available for future help.

If life throws a stressful or traumatic event in your path, or you have a mental-health diagnosis that needs maintenance care, avail yourself of every resource! If you can't shake a physical emotion or a nagging feeling, don't suffer in silence and think God is testing you. Talk with someone. Get counsel on what you're facing and be open to their suggestions.

For some, medication is a beneficial supplement to restore neurobiological health. We are embodied creatures whose genetics have been impacted by sin. Often the right dosage can give needed help to function well in daily life. There is no shame in seeking professional help.

I encourage you to not only be regularly disciplined with your attention but in your emotional life too, for working out your feelings honors a major part of what it means to be human, and it ultimately helps you grow in love for God and others.

DISCUSSION QUESTIONS

1. What has processing your emotions looked like for you in the past? What from this chapter has helped you better process your emotions?

2. In what ways does processing our emotions make us healthier, more mature Christians? In what ways does ignoring our emotions hold us back from Christian maturity?

3. Describe a time when you had an emotional response to a situation in your life. How did your body react? Use the Feelings Wheel on page 112 to further describe this moment.

4. As you process your emotions, what tends to be most difficult—expressing, naming, or discussing them with others? How might you seek to grow in this area?

5. The author recommended scheduling four blocks of time throughout your day for reflection and processing. How might this practice shift your overall view of God's presence in your life?

6. Practice sharing your story and asking others to share theirs. How do you see God at work?

7. Do you have a conversation partner who calls you to confess your sin and walk in the light? If not, how can you start pursuing a relationship like this in the next week?

CHAPTER 8

Trust God with *Every* Emotion

IN THE LAST CHAPTER, we discussed how important it is to be disciplined in processing our emotions. We also discussed various practices we can implement to get better at doing this; for when we do, we become healthier Christians overall.

That's all well and good, but the truth of the matter is that many of us do this in lopsided ways. We are comfortable enough to identify *some* emotions that rise up in our lives while looking the other way when our feelings take a form we feel embarrassed or shamed by, or even those that seem foreign to us.

For example, those who like to be happy will claim words like *joy* but never *bitter,* even if we indeed feel bitter sometimes. For those with a melancholy disposition, we'll claim words like *sad* but rarely *enthusiastic,* even if a momentary buzz of excitement does rise up in us for some reason. For those who have a temper, we're okay to admit "we're frustrated," but we're afraid to admit that underneath all that anger is deep *sadness* or a sense of *betrayal*.

Or, for those who are decently conversant in emotional language, we might use words all over the spectrum, but we, too, hold back certain feelings from God, hoping to look strong instead of weak. We'll say we're *upset* when really we're *furious*. We're okay with words like *lonely* but certainly not *jealous or resentful of my friend who has everything I want*. We'll say we're *self-conscious* about that incident at the party but not *embarrassed* or *humiliated*. We're fine with *struggling* but not *floundering*. We'll even say *glad* or *thankful* or *humbled* when really we're feeling *over-the-moon elated* because we believe deep down if we enjoy something too much God will take it away.

For whatever reason and whatever our disposition, we know we should process our emotions with God, but a lot of times, we don't just say it like it is in His presence. We think the tornado of feelings that swirls around inside can be managed if we hold to one, maybe two, primary emotions and call it a day.

But that's just the thing. We are all, at any given moment, holding in a mix of emotions. Some light, some heavy, some in-between. Each of us carries both joy and pain, loss and ambition, hurt and hope. No one is as put together as they seem. I've been told that psychologically we can't shut off one part of our unpleasant feelings (like sadness) without also shutting off the pleasurable feelings (like happiness). It takes courage and a steady supply of mercy not just to expose our wounds, but for our wounds to be healed from the inside out. It also takes faith to celebrate without fearing the other shoe will drop. Good and bad, we must admit it all.

Parts of the contemporary evangelical church would do well to embrace the minor keys of the Christian life, recognizing and practicing grief, lament, and pain. At the same time, there are parts that need to practice celebration, rejoicing in God's provision and living with confident hope. We can trust God with the full spectrum of our emotions.

Just look at the Scriptures and see the conversations God has. Jeremiah laments that God seemingly tricked him (Jer. 20); Job mourns and asks hard questions (Job 3–31); Mary, full of tears, wails about Jesus being too late to help her brother Lazarus (John 11). In every one of these scenarios, the Lord does not run away wringing His hands, wondering what He's going to do with these massive emotions. Instead, He engages in conversation. Some of us think good Christians aren't allowed to feel sadness, depression, or doubt because God will be disappointed we don't have stronger faith. Better just to think them to ourselves (or post on social media). On the flip side, we think God might be equally disappointed if we're too excited about something. Yet, God doesn't expect us to be put together all the time or stoic in the way we experience life. We put that expectation on ourselves.

What God wants to do is engage us in dialogue when we aren't put together, just as He did with all these biblical characters.

God is big enough to handle you being in process. He's big enough for you to make a mess and need help. He's big enough to love you when you won't love yourself. We just need to show up with all our baggage and our birthday candles, trusting Him to deal with us rightly in every circumstance because He's a good father who gives Himself (Luke 11:1–13), and all things work together for our good (Rom. 8).

I'm not saying we shouldn't seek to grow more sanctified in our emotional life. Indeed, we want to become more godly in all areas of our life, including our emotions. We don't want to spend our days utterly consumed with jealousy, rivalry, contempt, or malice, for example. What I *am* saying is that you're not going to get very far down the path of Christian maturity in your emotional life if you don't bring *every* emotion to Him—the ones you're comfortable with admitting *and* the ones you're not. You've got to get honest and disciplined with God here, regularly offering up your emotions to Him—every single one of them—trusting Him to help you and change you. We all must do this if we're serious about growing as a Christian.

This has been a hard thing for me to learn, so I'll share some ideas for disciplining yourself to bring every emotion to God.

PRAY THE PSALMS

The Psalms help us know how to put words to our hearts because the psalms are answering speech.[1] Calvin called the psalms "An Anatomy of all the Parts of the Soul," saying, "there is not an emotion of which anyone can be conscious that is not here represented as in a mirror. Or rather, the Holy Spirit has here drawn to the life all the griefs, sorrows, fears, doubts, hopes, cares, perplexities—in short, all the distracting emotions with which the minds of men are wont to be agitated."[2]

The Psalms cover the spectrum of human experience. Written over a thousand-year period, they engage lament, grief, joy, confidence, praise, and despair. The collection of songs play a vital role in the memory of God's people as they rehearse the work of God. The psalms give space for thoughts, emotions, and actions to come before God in prayer. One of my favorite authors says that "to remember the past is to see that we are here today by grace, that we have survived as a gift."[3] The Psalms provoke their readers to remember the grace of today and the gift of survival. We all have moments we were not sure we could make it through, but here we are by grace.

When you're not sure what or how to pray, the Psalms have you covered. Praying through the Psalms on a regular basis helps you be reminded of the goodness of God and see how God has received the emotions of His people through history. They give words to what we can't name and make space for the Spirit to groan on our behalf (Rom. 8:26–27).

During my time at Southern Seminary, Donald Whitney taught a method for praying the psalms that has stuck with me. It's from his book, *Praying the Bible*. Here's the method: scan five psalms a day and pray through the one that resonates with you in the moment.[4] It's not rocket science, and you can jump in at any time. You'll cover the whole book of Psalms in a month, and you might not pray through the same psalm again for months.

Want to see how this might look in your own prayer time? Watch how Whitney walks you through an example with the first verses of Psalm 20.

> So you might read the beginning of verse 1 [ESV]—"May the LORD answer you in the day of trouble!"—and pray:
>
> *Lord, please answer me today. I am in trouble—my finances are in trouble, my body is in trouble, and my relationships are in trouble. O answer me today, Lord, because I am in trouble in so many ways.*
>
> Then you read the second half of verse 1 [ESV]: "May the name of Jacob's God protect you!" That prompts you to pray something like this:

> *Thank you, God of Jacob, that through your Son, Jesus, you have set me securely on high by your grace. I will never fall. By your work of preserving me through the Holy Spirit, I am securely set on high. The Bible says in Ephesians that I am seated in the heavenly places with Christ. Thank you for the security of that and all you have done for me in Christ.*[5]

In praying through the Psalms, we're joining a discipline the people of God have used for thousands of years, offering them, and all the emotions they entail, up to the One who created them.

LIVE THE PSALMS

Live the Psalms? Yes, live them by bringing all of who we are before God. We place a high value on learning, but if the learning only lives in our thoughts and doesn't serve our whole selves, we miss the embodied nature of our life with God. We are not only our brains on sticks; our bodies matter too. Expressing grief and joy is imperative to processing life and learning to trust God at work in a broken world. So, how might we live the Psalms? Here are two ways.

Live the Psalms by Trusting God with Lament

There is a space between pain and promise that we often skip over because we believe being a good Christian means you can't feel your sad emotions too deeply. The Bible has a word for it: *lament.* In *Dark Clouds, Deep Mercy*, Mark Vroegop defines this space of lament as the honest cry of a hurting heart wrestling with the paradox of pain and the promise of God's goodness.[6]

The world wants to fix sadness rather than feel it. If we are willing to see it, the Christian life is one of continual lament *and* joy. We live with questions of pain, suffering, loss, and unfulfilled desire as we have faith in the promise of God's goodness. In fact, one-third of the psalms are lament. Our experience is not unique but human.

To lament is to risk living with one's deepest questions unanswered. But it is to ask them, and you need to know that it's okay to ask them. This is how we trust God with the reality of our pain in the hope of His promise.[7]

The church holds space for the hurting. The gospel makes it possible for us to want things to change and hold firm hope that one day they ultimately will. Sandra McCracken, a music minister, singer-songwriter and author, adds: "Our culture is uncomfortable with extended grief. The church has a responsibility to fight against the dishonesty of living on the surface of things, or encouraging people to put a smile on their faces so they will have a positive attitude about difficult things."[8]

Are you tempted to believe God can't handle your grief? Think your disappointment is too much for Him? Have the people of God failed to understand why you're stuck in the space between pain and promise? We need to both trust God and learn to trust His people with our grief and lament. We are meant to bear each other's burdens. We mourn with those who mourn, and when we don't understand why our family is mourning, we get down next to them in the dark until we can see from their point of view.

Live the Psalms by Sitting with the Hurting

When things are deeply broken and we are powerless to change them, we need God to make it right. This is the heart of lament not just when we're trusting God to help us for some issue going on in our lives, but in the lives of those around us.

When you see others hurting, sit with them and let yourself become uncomfortable for the same reason they are. Name what's wrong, mourn that it exists, and pray for God to make it right. Enter into their lament and seek to understand how to pray for them, the situation, and what it might look like for God to act. Be like Job's friends and mourn with them (Job 2:11–13)—but maybe lay off the trite advice.

An example from contemporary history is to recognize the lament of many ethnicities regarding their mistreatment based on perceived otherness, a demeaning of their equality of being made in God's image as a person. To recognize pain and promise, we mourn the mistreatment of humanity by humanity, and we ask God to fulfill His reconciling work of humanity to Himself, within Himself, and to one another. Where we have opportunity and relationship to be present in this conversation, it is both ministry and discipline. We must engage hard things instead of avoiding them.

As the book of Job and many of the psalms show us, lament alongside a friend pleads with God to make things right in their situation, recognizing His original design for the world's flourishing and our fallen experience are not matching up. We fight cynicism in our prayers for our friends by lamenting in hope. We voice our frustration over their plight and admit our need for God's hand to move while reminding ourselves and our friend that God is good and to be trusted.

Live the Psalms in Worship and at the Table

In a culture that downplays physical presence and praises digital connection, the church offers a distinctly countercultural community. Gathering together as Christians helps us bring our whole selves before God and one another. We confess our need, sing our hope, hear our salvation, and remind ourselves what is true. A healthy church body is one who doesn't avoid pain but works to see it healed, *together*.[9] Let's not forget the psalms are the notes to the soundtrack of Israel's life with God, and many of them were used in corporate settings. We lament through song because, in singing, the community confesses our inability to fix things. McCracken comments:

> I am convinced that the songs that we sing have a role in shaping our hearts, and songs of lament can make space for us to feel more deeply and to speak more honestly before God. We need songs of lament to be part of our church life, every week. In doing so, I hope that we would not be held fast in our complacency, but drawn out of hiding and comforted by our loving, pursuing Father.[10]

Since the Protestant Reformation, the Sunday sermon has become the height of the service for many. If your tradition practices Communion or the Lord's Supper, this is the historical center of the Christian worship service. Coming around the table as a family is to gather as exiles in a foreign land, prodigal sinners made saints. It is to be met by the risen Christ in the power of the Holy Spirit as we put our faith in the food He has provided for us *together*. The supper is where we engage with our *whole* selves in the service. We physically eat and drink reminders of Christ's provision for us at a shared table with a community forged (and kept) by grace. We think upon Christ, look around at the table, and remind ourselves things are not yet finished. Returning to the table again and again reminds us to proclaim our hope. It displays our inability to fix the broken things and rather fixes our eyes on God, who has promised that He will do so in the end. We eat and drink in lament and hope *together*. The table reminds us of the reality of the kingdom and calls us to pattern our lives after it with all we are—with our attention, our emotions, and our limits.

Live the Psalms by Practicing Celebration

Years ago I heard the following illustration:

> Christmas Eve. Beautiful night. Light snowfall. Young family of four in the car, on the way to grandma's house for dinner. They're listening to the radio station, the one that starts playing the Christmas music like right at Halloween. "Jingle Bells" comes on. The kids in the back seat go crazy. Everyone breaks into song. The camera pans in on the faces of the kids, the mom, dad. . . .
>
> What happens next?[11]

Your answer?

The speaker went on: "60 percent of people say 'car crash.' Sixty percent. Another 10 percent to 15 percent have equally fatalistic answers, but more creative."[12]

How many of us live our lives this way—expecting something bad to happen so we protect ourselves from expecting joy? What happens to the human heart (Christian or not) when we think expecting the worst is better than hoping for the good?

The remedy for a worst-case-scenario posture is celebration. For the joy of our hearts we need to celebrate God, His specific provision, and His presence in daily life. *Everything we have* and *everyone in our lives* is a gift of grace. Life with God is an invitation to delight in God's truth, goodness, and beauty toward us in the highs, lows, and Mondays of life because we've been reconciled to the family. We protect ourselves by clamping a ceiling on our delight, where God wants to lead us further into joy through life with Him.

The discipline of living the psalms through celebration is to believe that we are children of our Father, and children belong with their father.[13] "Grace lets you be who you are supposed to be even though you do not deserve to or may not want to."[14] When we practice celebration, look for grace and actively notice God's provision each day, and thereby root ourselves in God's grace and in joy. This kind of joy "is not an optional feature of the faith, nor can it be attained by smiling more and singing louder. It must emerge from an awareness of the mercy and forgiveness of God enacted in the Kingdom."[15]

Emotional maturity is a necessity for the follower of Christ. Learning how to process and move through our emotions is key to living in God's reality, including the emotions you'd rather not offer up to Him or the ones you'd rather not walk through with others. Remember in this hard work that God has given us Christ, who has received us in our imperfection, no matter the mess we find ourselves in, always offering us a better path to walk down. Trust God with all of who you are, Christian. Lament, celebrate, and stay connected to the body of Christ. If we discipline ourselves in the years of plenty when it comes to our emotions, we will find ourselves nourished and resilient against the drought of cynicism and doubt in God's goodness. And we will find we are healthier, more mature, and able to help those in need.

DISCUSSION QUESTIONS

1. What emotions do you feel most comfortable expressing to God? Think through the vocabulary you use often with Him. What words often come out when you seek Him in prayer? (For example, words like *overwhelmed*, *frustrated*, *sad*, *upset*, *confused*, etc.)

2. What emotions do you have the hardest time expressing? Which ones do you hold back or perhaps try to cloak in better language to seem stronger?

3. In what ways have you avoided the practice of lament? In what ways have you avoided the practice of celebration? Why?

4. What does it mean to "pray the psalms"? Have you ever tried this? What about praying the psalms seems comforting to you? Challenging to you?

5. Practice praying a psalm. How does this psalm give voice to your emotions?

6. What does it look like to cultivate celebration in your daily life? How can you look for grace and actively notice God's provision each day? Consider what it might look like to celebrate important milestones with those around you, how you might name and celebrate God's good gifts, and how you might record these moments, whether in a file or journal or through photos.

7. Both the Lord's Supper and meals together with other believers model what is to come. Is there space in your current weekly schedule for you to eat a meal with others often, seeking

intentional conversation about what God is doing? If not, how might you make space?

DIMENSION THREE

Disciplining Our Limits

I don't like the man who doesn't sleep, says God.
Sleep is the friend of man.
Sleep is the friend of God.
Sleep is perhaps the most beautiful thing I have created,
and I myself rested on the seventh day.
He whose heart is pure, sleeps, And he who sleeps has a pure heart.
That is the great secret of being as indefatigable as a child,
of having that strength in legs that a child has.
Those new legs, those new souls,
And to begin afresh every morning, ever new.
Like young hope, new hope.
But they tell me that there are men

Who work well and sleep badly.
Who don't sleep. What a lack of confidence in me.

I pity them. I have it against them. A little, they don't trust me.
Like the child who innocently lies in her mother's arms, thus they do not lie
Innocently in the arms of my Providence.
They have the courage to work. They haven't enough virtue to be idle.
To stretch out. To rest. To sleep.
Poor people, they don't know what is good.
They look after their business very well during the day.

But they haven't enough confidence in me to let me look after it during the night.
As if I wasn't capable of looking after it during one night.
He who doesn't sleep is unfaithful to Hope.
And it is the greatest infidelity.[1]

CHAPTER 9

Embrace Your Creaturehood

IN OUR JOURNEY TOWARD our future self, we've covered why our attention and emotions are important to bring before God in a disciplined way of life. Now it is time to explore a final (and typically overlooked) category of discipline for becoming healthy Christians: our limits.

Why limits? Because for all our strengths, surrendering to God's good design inherently points to the borders of our lives that He has deemed best. In this section, we will consider three ways to engage our limits: *embracing our creaturehood, living with the end in mind,* and *living into community.* All of these encourage us to trust God is who He says He is: in control.

Remember King Solomon? One night God says to him in a dream: "What can I give you?" Solomon says, "Here's what I want: Give me a God-listening heart so I can lead your people well, discerning the difference between good and evil. For who on their own is capable of leading your glorious people?" (1 King 3:5, 9 MSG).

God gave Solomon a blank check, and Solomon asked for a discerning, God-listening heart. He asked for wisdom. God's response to Solomon was to grant a wise and mature heart among other blessings.

The question reappears from the mouth of Jesus in many gospel accounts: "What do you want me to do for you?"[1]

My response? I want wisdom, Lord. How else will I know the difference between good and evil, right and wrong, in this life? I want a God-listening heart because I'm tired of listening to myself.

Are you tired of listening to yourself?

Our world has traded God's wisdom for our feelings and access to information. The Internet in our pocket has leveled the value of experience and expertise. But access to information does not equal character transformation. Facts are not wisdom. Wisdom is the application of discernment to circumstances in pursuit of the good and beautiful life with God, and wisdom is found in God.

When met with the gap between who we want to be and who we actually are, the wisdom of the world tells us to change our beliefs to accommodate our desires rather than change our desires to match our beliefs. Our innate preference for self corrupts our sense of delight in the true, the good, and the beautiful

(Rom. 1). We pursue a God-listening heart by ordering our lives according to God's good design, which enables us to delight in God over the world.[2]

James tells us that there is wisdom from below and from above. The Teacher in Ecclesiastes calls it wisdom from under and over the sun. There is wisdom that is not wisdom because it comes from the creation. There is wisdom from the Creator, and this wisdom brings true life on *His* terms, not ours. Only when we acknowledge our limits, embrace our creaturehood, and lean entirely on the Lord may we have wisdom. Our days are numbered as those created by the Creator, and we want to live these given days with wisdom.

The psalmist tells us: "The fear of the LORD is the beginning of wisdom" (Ps. 111:10). If you'd allow me a paraphrase, I'd say it this way: *The beginning of wisdom is to desire a God-listening heart.*

Years ago I fell into a couch, looked at the counselor in front of me, and sighed. *I know there will always be work to do, but it's the fact that I want to work all the time that's bothering me. I have one gear and it's set to achieve. I need the busyness to feel okay, and it's taking life from me.*

During this season, I was in my second year of PhD coursework. Every Tuesday evening, I put our kids to bed, said goodnight to Carly, and grabbed a booth at an all-night diner from 9:00 p.m. to 4:00 a.m.

I'd read about four hundred pages of church history and down too much motor oil masquerading as coffee. Then I'd make the drive home to sleep. Up with the kids at 6:30, in class at 8:30 to cover said reading, and then off to my full-time pastoral role for the rest of the week. This cycle repeated weekly for a year.

Truth be told, it felt good to grind like that. I thought I could be all things: a husband, dad, pastor, PhD student. If I just worked hard enough, I wouldn't have to let go of anything. I cherished my ability to overfunction.

Then I read this:

> Putting wise limits upon our undertakings and our spheres is one of the most important and anxious things that we have to do. And one of the chief modern sins is attempting too much, and not being willing to keep ourselves strictly within the limits of what we can do really well. The young man thinks he can do anything and everything; and it may often be the consequence that he does nothing really well.[3]

Seems like I wanted wisdom, just not as much as I wanted to deny my creaturehood. I had no patience for dependence or limits because I live in a world of independence and self-sufficiency.

In the midst of this, I encountered Psalm 131. Three little verses that will change your life.

> LORD, my heart is not proud;
> my eyes are not haughty.
> I do not get involved with things
> too great or too wondrous for me.
> Instead, I have calmed and quieted my soul
> like a weaned child with its mother;
> my soul is like a weaned child.
>
> Israel, put your hope in the LORD,
> both now and forever.

In the context of denying our creaturehood, David Powlison takes Psalm 131 and flips it to reveal the functional belief under our actions:

> Self, my heart is proud (I'm absorbed in myself),
> and my eyes are haughty (I look down on other people),
> and I chase after things too great and too difficult for me.
> So of course I'm noisy and restless inside, it comes naturally,
> like a hungry infant fussing on his mother's lap,
> like a hungry infant, I'm restless with my demands and worries.
> I scatter my hopes onto anything and everybody all the time.[4]

Knowing our God-designed limits and embracing our creaturehood is something we rail against. It feels like death, and it is. It's death to our pride and the lie that we are self-sufficient.

Are you constantly hoping the next achievement, purchase, or person will finally quiet the noise of your heart? Instead of embracing our vocation as creatures, we have embraced the vocation of consumer by chasing freedom from limits.[5] We keep defining ourselves outside of our creaturehood. We live in a day where saying, "I am one who is made in the image of God," is a foreign concept, but proclaiming, "I am my genes, I am my [chosen] gender, I am what I do, what I have, or who I love," are all prized and self-constructed ways to making sense of the impact of sin on our hearts (mind, emotions, and actions) and the corruption of our ability to see reality clearly.[6]

In my dad's office when I was growing up was a quote from William James: "Nothing is so fatiguing as the eternal hanging on of an unfinished task." As I've gotten more familiar with Psalm 131, I've learned that nothing is so fatiguing as eternally hanging onto things too great and too wondrous for me (v. 1). In every denial of rest, every comparison of what I've done versus what others have been given, with every denial of help and every space I seek my way over someone else's—I despise my created frame instead of embracing it. When I embrace my creaturehood, my soul exhales into calm waters by putting my hope in God because He cares for me.

Here are some disciplines you can practice in order to better embrace your creaturehood and offer up your limits to God on a regular basis.

PRACTICE SABBATH

The concept of the Sabbath has gone through a bit of revival in the last decade. Increasing numbers of companies have begun to offer paid sabbaticals, and people talk about needing a Sabbath to recover from the stress and anxiety of daily life. It has come to mean a day off, time alone, or whatever constitutes self-care, which is a Western definition of Sabbath, not a biblical one.

The American Sabbath is an escape at the end of a busy week. We spend the week serving the autonomous self, building our own kingdoms, or simply grinding to make ends meet. How many of us spend our days to earn future rest, only to not know how to be present when it comes?

You might be tempted to think Sabbath is your earned rest, but the Sabbath is not merely a day off. It's not a form of retreat but of resistance. It's not just resistance; it's rehearsal. The Sabbath is not self-care but self-denial.[7]

Rest in God is *active* rest. It is resistance to the false stories of this age, and it is a rehearsal of the true story of God. Like those before us, when we distrust that God is who He says He is and what He says about us is true, we need His help to remember we are not gods ourselves.

God restored Israel's freedom out from under Pharoah with a call to embrace creaturely limits by resisting hurry, anxiety, and restlessness. The Sabbath is to remind us who He is and who we really are: people He loves who bear His image.

Many of us willingly live under the rule of hurry, anxiety, and restlessness. We are working to provide for ourselves, constantly comparing with the lives of those around us. Yet God gives us the Sabbath to interrupt this pattern and remind us to remember that He is God and we are not. He's the One who doesn't sleep so we can rest in peace.

We're addicted to achievement and accumulating because we refuse to be content with *who* we've been given and the *worth* we've been given by Him. We're addicted to self. We love the idea that we can control our future through health, fitness, safety, money, and morality. We'll sing songs declaring our sinfulness and praising God's goodness, then we'll calendar like the world is on our shoulders. We search for a day off when what we need is a Sabbath—time spent actively denying the urge to produce and humbling our hearts before God. Sabbath restores our sight.

In Christ, the Sabbath stands as a gift to remember that God is our Creator, and He knows best (Heb. 4). We delight in God and His work with an ever-increasing joy. We strive and train for our future rest by practicing Sabbath now. We cultivate delight in God for who He is and what He's done, to remind us that He's our Creator and He cares for us. We sabbath to proclaim that we are *in* Christ.

> Because of Christ, you are free from hurry. He's provided for you.
>
> Because of Christ, you are free from anxiety. You can trust Him.
>
> Because of Christ, you are free to rest. True contentment is yours in Him alone.

So, dear Christian, practice God's gift of Sabbath. You will not grow in your love for God as your Creator if you don't get in weekly rhythms of *feeling* your creaturehood. There are no shortcuts to spiritual maturity in this area, for Sabbath forces dependence on the Creator, and dependence is a hallmark trait of the mature believer.

Sunset to Sunset

When do you think the day starts? 5:00 a.m.? 7:00 a.m.? 9:00 a.m.? Days in biblical times didn't start at midnight but at sunset. If we consider sunset the start, we go to sleep and wake up in the same day where God has not slept, but He's kept you. Sabbath has historically been the setting aside of a day—sunset to sunset—to actively rest, remember, and rejoice in who God is. It might include spending time walking or tending a garden, reading a book, building something with your hands, or being with friends. Ceasing work reminds us that we have a Maker and He has met our needs in full.

We also live in a world that believes in self-sufficiency and self-reliance, but we cannot do the Christian life alone. The presence of others helps pull us out of ourselves and reorient us to the true story. Sabbath was and is meant to foster depth of life and worship of God in community. Sabbath is a day for the people of God to remember their creaturehood and honor their Creator *together*.

What might Sabbath practically look like? Here's what we've done the last few years (given that I work on Sundays, we start a little early):

Around dinner on Friday, phones get put away. The family eats together and watches a movie. We laugh, dance to cartoons, and eat ice cream. Everyone heads to bed, and Saturday starts with coffee for the adults and books for all. After breakfast, we might go for a walk, swim, play games, or build with Legos. The focus is being present to God and one another during the day. We are *together*.

Most weekends we rotate homes between three families for Saturday dinner. We cook a meal together as the kids run, then we share food and conversation meant to cultivate gratitude and praise to God for who He is and what He's done. We play games, enjoy one another, and laugh. We clean up, head home, and sleep knowing that we're kept by our Maker.

Sunday we wake up, and in the crazy of getting three little humans to church, we come to praise God and rehearse reality with the family of God.

Develop your own rhythms of Sabbath and embrace it as a sweet gift from God, who works on our behalf even when we are still. Prepare for it, guard it, and live from the gift of rest rather than for it.

LIVE WITHIN YOUR LIMITS

The world tells us: you can be whatever you want to be. Believing the world, we chase what we can provide for ourselves. We ignore (even disdain) our limits because they remind us we are not self-sufficient, self-sustaining, and self-reliant. It's a creature's reach to be the Creator, and it's not new. We've been doing it since the garden of Eden. This is part of us. Limits are God's way of showing us how to live the good life as finite, created beings. We call limits weakness and God calls them wisdom.

You have been given a particular body with talents, gifts, and privileges to steward. But you have also been given limits. Limits are a mercy to remind us we're not the Creator. I can't run near as fast as I'd like, and I get cranky when hungry. When I live in a way that overfunctions, I'm testing my limits instead of believing that true rest is in embracing creaturehood. The limits of everyday life remind us we're not the one who sustains life. Trusting we don't have to produce to be loved or accepted by God, we are free to stop trying to earn both from other people by living outside our design.

It's one thing to agree with all these things in theory when it comes to our limits; it's another thing to *live out* that agreement. In what ways are you aware of your limits but still continuing to test them? In what ways are you refusing to live within the boundaries of being human, trying to live instead like a machine? What needs to change so that you can live what you say you believe about being a creature and not the Creator?

CONSIDER YOUR LIMITS

Perhaps there's a reason you're not living your limitations the way you should: you haven't actually considered them. After all, no one wants to feel inadequate. Whether that's through our bank account, physical fitness, health, our kid's accomplishments, or what we can provide at large, we don't like to feel limited. The engine of consumerism and the champions of human ability don't want you to feel limited. They don't even want you *thinking* about your limitations, actually, which explains (at least in part) why most of us don't think often about them. But limited is exactly what we are.

As a discipline, regularly consider your limited, finite nature. Ponder passages like Psalm 103:13–14 on a regular basis, meditating on its teaching that indeed "we are only dust," but also that God is our compassionate Father who takes care of us in our frailty:

> The LORD is like a father to his children,
> tender and compassionate to those who fear him.
> For he knows how weak we are;
> he remembers we are only dust. (NLT)

As you ponder your finite nature, consider the responsibilities, roles, and relationships you hold in daily life. Name the pressures you feel each day, the demands on your attention and time. Pray and seek to discern what is an expectation from the world versus a gift from the Lord. Taking time to name our limits in this way helps us come to terms with our creaturehood and drives us to dependance on God, the Giver of help and life. There are limits to every part of our life, and as you practice the discipline of regularly considering them, you'll grow in your ability to see them less as killjoys and more as protective borders of human flourishing. You'll grow into a Christian who believes the grass truly is greener inside God's good design.

FOCUS ON THE PRESENT

As I mentioned earlier, one of my disciplines each morning is to think and pray through the day to come. The calendar is planned far ahead of time to structure responsibilities and commitments in each dimension of life. I do this so that I can be as prepared as possible for what that future moment might bring.

The lie of having no limits is that we will always have more time. More time to try again, more time for second and third chances, to say I'm sorry and catch up on what we put off because we were distracted. But the truth is that time is limited, and that's good.

Of course we should plan for the future. Yet we also need to practice living in the only moment we have any say over—right now.

Sometimes I write in the mornings before my kids are awake. Recently my son came downstairs well ahead of the agreed-upon time. He was dressed for school and eager for the day. My initial internal response was frustration that my productive time was being interrupted. I asked him to sit next to me and read while I finished up, and he did just that. Over the next half hour, with my son sitting next to me, I thought of a list I read years ago. Philosopher Albert Borgmann has four affirmations that help him focus his attention on what matters most:

> There is no place I would rather be.
> There is nothing I would rather do.
> There is no one I would rather be with.
> This I will remember well.[8]

In his book *Living into Focus,* Arthur Boers comments on Borgmann's list:

> I want to live in a way that enables me to offer these focal affirmations often. I want to fully be where I am. I want to wholeheartedly do what I am doing. I want to intentionally spend time with the people around me. I want to spend my days in ways worth remembering. While complicated and challenging, living a life with focal affirmations in view is not impossible.[9]

I looked over at my son that morning in all his six-year-old glory, and those four affirmations rang true in the depths of my heart. Yes, there were things to do, but there was no place I would rather be, nothing else I would rather do, no one I would rather be with, and I will remember those quiet moments well.

I'm not sure how you tend to avoid the present. Maybe there are certain times of day you dwell on memories of the past or certain practices in your week that focus all your energy toward the future. I'm not saying those moments in your week are bad, but take some time to identify where those moments might be crowding your ability to focus on the present. At what crucial moments might you be present in body but *gone* mentally or emotionally, living in some other moment? What could help you return to *right now* and savor it? Perhaps you're afraid to return to the present moment because you're afraid you'll lose a thought that's important—so your answer might be to keep a notebook nearby so you can jot down the thought and get to it later. Maybe you have a hard time dialing into the moment because you are replaying past conversations over and over on a loop, and what you need to do in those moments is step away, pray, release it to God as the keeper of the past, and return to the present moment He's asking you to steward. However it needs to look for you, find a couple of practices that will help you return to *right now.* As you make this a habit, you'll grow in your ability to trust God as the only eternal One who can exist in all times and places at once, and you'll grow more and more free about the fact that you cannot.

DISCUSSION QUESTIONS

1. What limits in your life are especially frustrating for you? Why do you think these are the ones that rise to the top of the list for you?

2. What is wisdom? How do you get it?

3. In what ways do you deny your limitedness and seek to press beyond it? How does that normally go? When tempted in this way, how might you fight back with what you know now?

4. What Sabbath rhythms are in place in your life? How do you normally spend this time? What adjustments should be made so that you are actively resting and remembering God's goodness and provision during this time?

5. In what ways do you avoid the present? When you are mentally or emotionally detached from "right now," do you tend to focus more on the past or the future? Why?

6. What are some practices you can put in place to better embrace your creaturehood and focus on the present?

7. Return to the list of Borgmann's affirmations on page 157. Which of these four do you struggle with the most? How can you remember these truths?

CHAPTER 10

Live with the End in Mind

THIS MIGHT SOUND STRANGE, but I grew up around death.

In grade school, my mom and I made regular trips to the nursing home. The moments were familiar: the warmth of fresh bread on the drive as Mom brought something familiar to those in unfamiliar spaces. In my mind, the smells of the hospice wing mix with popcorn in the lobby. This same lobby would welcome my grandfather before cancer took him in my high school years. Seared in that same mind live the words of Mike, my seventh-grade Sunday school teacher whom I visited after my college years and his cancer treatments were nearly finished. He smiled and said, "I'm going home, Mason."

I was halfway across the world when I heard Mom's voicemail: *I need to hear your voice; please call me. We need to talk.* The news of Dad's tumors brought me to the ground. These days, my parents, sister, and I celebrate every family dinner because many days we weren't sure we'd have another to share.

This brings us to the Latin phrase, *Memento Mori.* In English, it translates: *Remember you must die.* Ready for that tattoo now? Death is part of life, and most of us are doing our best to ignore it altogether. But living with the end in mind fuels Christian hope.

Artists throughout history have placed skulls on desks of theologians, philosophers, and saints. These secondhand heads are visual cues to think about the brevity of life and certainty of death. Christians contemplate death to live in reality. If we ignore death, we deny the power of Christ's defeat of death and our resurrection hope. I regularly exercise, pay attention to my diet, and have been known to buy more than a few vitamins. I also attend every funeral I can and take my kids. Facing our mortality brings the larger questions into focus. It might seem sad, but soberness is not the enemy of joy. Contemplating your own death can lead to delight in Christ. If the Lord tarries, one day His tomb won't be the only one empty.

Memento mori brings awareness that we're not in control of our lives and could shuffle off this mortal coil at any point.[1] If we act like death will never come, we will live like there is always more time and another chance. "Yet you do not know what tomorrow will bring—what your life will be! For you are like vapor that appears for a little while, then vanishes" (James 4:14).

After receiving his cancer diagnosis and being told to put his affairs in order, Steve Jobs told others it meant, "to try to tell your kids everything you thought you'd have the next ten years to tell them in just a few months. It means to make sure everything is buttoned up so that it will be as easy as possible for your family. It means to say your goodbyes."[2]

These days I tell my wife and kids I love them every day, multiple times a day. I call my parents, and I say the things you save for special occasions because life together is special enough. I text my sister I'm proud of her and thankful for our friendship. I want my people to never guess what I thought of them so they can hear my voice and read my words long after I'm with Christ. As Christians, we seek to leave nothing unsaid or undone.

Jonathan Edwards said it well in his resolutions:

> 7. Resolved, never to do anything, which I should be afraid to do, if it were the last hour of my life.[3]

That might provoke images of a street evangelist asking where you would go if you die tonight. If you're in Christ, the question shifts: *What have I left undone before the Lord and others?* A seemingly morbid rhythm becomes fertile soil for hope and holiness. We don't need to fear death; we need to live in light of it.

How do we practice the discipline of *Memento Mori*? Well, you *could* put a skull on your desk, but regardless of the skull, you should absolutely think on death. In a culture that avoids death, we remember it's a reality for us. None escape it, but you can live well today by considering it and seeking to become the person you hope will be described at your funeral. David Brooks calls these descriptors the eulogy virtues. One of the benefits of remembering our death is to provide space for self-examination and see where Merton's quote—the one on page 13 that we started the book with—applies to our lives:

> Ask me what I think I am living for, in detail, and ask me what I think is keeping me from living fully the thing I want to live for. Between these two answers you can determine the identity of any person. The better answer he has, the more of a person he is.[4]

So, what are you living for? And what is keeping you from living fully in this way? What's being left unsaid or undone? Let these questions guide a regular rhythm for you. Provide yourself space and time to process the implications of these answers for the near future and then look ten, twenty, or thirty years down the road. Ask the Lord what He'd like you to do and who He'd like you to become, and listen.

Here are some ideas for disciplining yourself to live with the end in mind.

KEEP THE CALENDAR

In the kitchen of my childhood home, just above the phone, there was a calendar—the kind of paper ones sold now in seasonal stores, the kind the smart phone made obsolete. Countless times I walked by the hub of our home, and Mom would be standing there, tethered to the wall, looking at the squared-off pages and taking notes, cradling the phone with her shoulder.

Each year she'd unwrap a new calendar and transfer dates between them. Fifty-two weeks with decades of names, dates, and events from others' lives:

- the birth of friends' children
- the death of friends' loved ones and of our friends
- the birth of family and the death of family
- wedding anniversaries and church activities
- all amid the lives of two busy kids and the court calendar of my judge father

We were no strangers to the house of mourning, and it was the calendar my mom meticulously kept that quietly reminded us of the mourning of our brother or sister who could likely use a phone call to say: You are loved, you are not forgotten, and neither are they.

The nature of keeping the calendar—of minding events in the lives of others—is to consider their lives, joys, hurts, loneliness, despair, and withdrawal in their suffering. When the casseroles and calls end, the mourner is often forgotten. In our hurried world, caring for those made in God's image is not efficient. It is more often inconvenient to our own plans, but it is a ministry to others and a reminder that our lives are but a vapor.

ENTER THE HOUSE OF MOURNING

Regardless of the room or the faces before me, I have been in this house many times. The kitchen is piled high with dishes. Cards from friends sit next to a box of thank-you notes. Conversations are in hushed tones. Everyone's in the living room, one disappearing only to return and say, "He's okay, just sleeping."

The house of mourning is a sober and special place in the life of a Christian. It is a place to hold fast in hope, to grieve the sting of death. There are tears and laughter because it is an altogether human experience of emotions in the face of loss and hope.

Enter the house of mourning. Sit next to the hospital bed and hold a hand. Read Scripture to those who can no longer see. Pray for and sing over those who cannot speak. Be present.

A note to those who may be ministering to those walking through great mourning:

1. Realize that you can't always do it later. Show up when you can. Often what we think can't be moved will be just fine, and making time for others is worth it.
2. Don't be nervous around the sick and dying. Death is part of life and is something we must come to terms with. However, don't feel like you need to point out the silver lining. There is a right weight to the house of mourning. The writer of Ecclesiastes said: "It is better to go to a house of mourning than to go to a house of feasting, since that is the end of all mankind, and the living should take it to heart" (Eccles. 7:2).
3. Pray for the family, be sensitive to how long you stay, and proactively provide help. Asking people to *let them know if you can do anything* is less helpful than having food delivered or dropping something off and letting them handle it as they'd like.

DISCUSSION QUESTIONS

1. How might you wisely think on death often? What might need to change in your life to leave nothing unsaid or undone?

2. When you hear of the death of another, how do you pause to consider their life? How does this bring sobriety for how you are handling the gift of today?

3. How could you begin to "keep a calendar" of important dates for those you love? Develop a rhythm of recording these dates or setting reminders and sending a card or calling on those important days when they may feel most alone.

4. How can you be present with someone in their mourning? Consider showing up for a friend's surgery, or when they're in the hospital or in need of company. Consider how life goes on for those in grief and how you might encourage them as they develop a new normal. Give them the gift of presence.

CHAPTER 11

Live into Community

ON SATURDAY NIGHT I know what to expect: a loud house full of kids, three couples, and a home-cooked meal. It's family dinner, and I love it.

A couple of years ago we risked a potentially awkward conversation that felt a little like, "Hey, we all seem to get along. Can we be better friends?" It was middle school all over again.

Throughout this work I've talked about the impact of consumerism and the value of choice in our lives. Some of us have lost the ability to talk with people in person, preferring to have our phone buffer for us. We want to control how needy our interactions are—which is to say, deep down we value independence over belonging. We say we want to be known, but depth of friendship comes with limiting yourself from who's next to who's here. It's also committing to living in relationship with other people: their strengths, weaknesses, quirks, suffering, needs, and life as it comes. In friendship we forsake the many for the sake of the few.

Somewhere we convinced ourselves that it is better to be barely known by many than deeply by few. We can mistakenly think good Christians keep multiplying their home groups, saying goodbye to friends, and restarting relationships to make disciples. But we're not made to have thirty close friends. It's actually *healthy* to have a small group of friends who through trust, constancy, and time form a life together. We should all be so lucky to find a band of brothers and sisters to join in community.

The days are full, and friendship doesn't microwave well. Friendships take time and effort. In the last few years for our small crew, family members passed, cancer hit, jobs shifted, kids struggled, miscommunication happened. During it all, we've made life together a priority.

When there is conflict, it takes resolve to reconcile, rebuild, and move forward together. We learn to admit need, ask for help, and proactively meet the needs of others. Life together brings interruptions, encouragements, and interdependence as we use our gifts for the good of others. We only learn to be patient by having others be patient with us, and we learn to love by being loved. This necessitates healthy friendship, interdependence, and hospitality. I become more of who I hope to be through commitment to others, not independence from them.

I'm reminded often: God sees you, you are not alone, and we are here for one another. These are my neighbors and friends by divine circumstance, and the constancy of life together is a stabilizing force in my life. We care for one another, we honor one another by speaking what we know to be true about one another, and when one of us falters, the others are quick to point us to Jesus. Every spiritual discipline is improved and expanded by practicing it in community. We were not made for individualism; we were made for God-given family.

Now it goes without saying that doing life together is not the same thing as giving other people the place in your life that only God should have. We can only do life with other image bearers well when we understand and worship the One whose image they were made in—God's. Otherwise, we will end up putting a weight on others that only God Himself can carry—telling me who I really am. He is the one who ultimately forms our identity, both in an individual sense and a corporate sense.

Keeping this caveat in mind, Christian, practice the discipline of life together, however you can and whatever that looks like for you. Don't give up in the typical moments our culture does. Keep pressing through, and you'll see that you're maturing—that you're looking a whole lot like Jesus, who journeyed with the same friends for many years and who made time for the people right in front of Him.

This may look like weekly or monthly neighborhood gatherings. It may look like keeping a consistent dinner on the calendar with loved ones in your church. It may mean a regular breakfast with those people you keep saying "you just have to catch up with" but never do. The Spirit has likely already brought some faces to mind. Who are they? And how can you discipline yourself to experience life together with them?

DISCUSSION QUESTIONS

1. What typically holds you back from doing life together with those God has granted you a connection with?

2. In what ways do you see yourself prioritizing "who's next?" instead of "who's here?" How does this posture toward those in front of you offend God?

3. In what ways does the discipline of *life together* acknowledge your limits?

4. How might you begin practicing the discipline of *life together*? What steps do you need to take?

CONCLUSION

A Process of Becoming

IN 2013, I JOINED a small team to plant a church in my hometown. A few days before we laid carpet, I wrote a reminder on the exposed concrete just inside my office, a Rubicon to cross at the start of each workday: "Relying on God has to begin all over again every day as if nothing had yet been done."[1] A decade and a few offices later, this quote is still a threshold to my days.

Becoming a healthy Christian is a lifelong process of change, day by day. Our spiritual disciplines make up the nature of our discipleship to Jesus. It is the continual surrender of all of life to God's good design for identity, belonging, and purpose. Paul calls this "your true worship" (Rom. 12:1), and Jesus likens it to branches finding life on the vine (John 15). He is the vine and we are the branches; the branch only thrives connected to the vine. Our act of worship and our connection to the vine are daily habits of reliance on God. Jesus tells us that to love Him is to follow

His design for life (John 15:10), and Paul calls this keeping "in step with the Spirit" (Gal. 5:25).

While we need daily reminders to depend on God, Christ loves without a sticky note. Our union to Christ is an invitation to receive love rather than fight for God's attention. Habits of discipline in the Christian life are an *intentional returning* to God's reality until it is our *predominant way of being.* I say predominant because, this side of glory, we are never fully free from the presence and power of sin, but we are no longer slaves to it. The Holy Spirit is working out what God has worked into us through Christ. Our part is to abide, return, and remain in trusting relationship with Him. In this we are progressively renewed from the inside out.

This renewal takes place through our working out of our stories, seeing where God has been present at every turn. As we use spiritual disciplines to direct our attention, engage our emotions, and embrace creaturely limits in specific, repeated ways, we'll find that we're actually *participating* in life with God instead of living our spiritual lives on the sidelines. We'll find we're training for life with God and that we are loved and kept by the Father, Son, and Holy Spirit. We'll find that we're increasingly hearing His voice, seeing His hand at work, and trusting His heart over our own through the power of the Spirit, who helps us live out who we are truly becoming in Christ. Eventually, as we keep at it, we'll also realize that at some point along the way, we started doing these disciplines not out of duty but joy, for we've come to discover that God is who He says He is and that a whole life regularly offered up to Him is indeed the good life. Ultimately, we'll find that we've become more like Him too.

Healthy, vibrant, and like Christ. That's what a whole life disciplined in God's direction does for us. What are we waiting for?

Jonathan Edwards invites us again to consider that as Christ "is like a river, and as water refreshes, so Christ refreshes and satisfies the heart, and makes it rejoice. The tree that spreads out its roots by a river has enough water; as a tree planted by a river is never dry: so Christ is never exhausted."[2]

Spiritual disciplines are a means to become increasingly aware that God is who He says He is, and what He says about you is true. This is how we surrender all of life to God's good design for identity, belonging, and purpose: we plant our lives next to the only stream that will never fail. As we learned in the beginning of this book, God's not waiting around for a future version of you to love, and He has a future version of you in mind. This is the great work of our lives: living into what God has in store for us in Christ and, as we do, becoming more like Him.

Recommended Works

Historical Christian Figures

Athanasius. *On the Incarnation*. Yonkers, NY: St. Vladimir's Seminary Press, 2021.

Augustine. *Confessions*. Translated by Henry Chadwick. Oxford World's Classics. New York: Oxford University Press, 2009.

Bavinck, Herman. *Guidebook for Instruction in the Christian Religion*. Translated by Gregory Parker. Peabody, MA: Hendrickson Academic, 2022.

Boothe, Charles Octavius. *Plain Theology for Plain People*. Hamburg, Germany: Albatross Publishers, 2020.

Calvin, John. *Institutes of the Christian Religion*. Peabody, MA: Hendrickson Publishers, 2008.

Edwards, Jonathan. *Charity and Its Fruits: Living in Light of Love*. Edited by Kyle Strobel. Wheaton, IL: Crossway, 2012.

Elliot, Elisabeth. *Suffering Is Never for Nothing*. Nashville, TN: B&H Publishing, 2019.

Herbert, George. *The Complete English Works*. Everyman's Library Edition. New York: Everyman, 1995.

Luther, Martin, and Dr. Haroldo S. Camacho. *Martin Luther's Commentary on St. Paul's Epistle to the Galatians*. Minneapolis, MN: 1517 Publishing, 2018.

Owen, John. *Overcoming Sin and Temptation*. Edited by Kelly M. Kapic and Justin Taylor. Wheaton, IL: Crossway, 2015.

Schaeffer, Francis. *True Spirituality*. Carol Stream, IL: Tyndale House, 1971.

Ten Boom, Corrie. *The Hiding Place: The Triumphant True Story of Corrie Ten Boom*. New York: Bantam Books, 1974.

Ryle, J. C. *Holiness*. Carlisle, PA: Banner of Truth, 2017.

Sayers, Dorothy L. *Are Women Human?* Grand Rapids: Eerdmans, 2005.

———. *Letters to a Diminished Church: Passionate Argument for the Relevance of Christian Doctrine*. Nashville, TN: Thomas Nelson, 2004.

Tada, Joni Eareckson. *When God Weeps*. Grand Rapids, MI: Zondervan, 2000.

Contemporary Works on Spiritual Formation and Disciplines

Adams, Isaac. *Talking about Race: Gospel Hope for Hard Conversations*. Grand Rapids, MI: Zondervan, 2022.

Barton, Ruth Haley. *Sacred Rhythms: Arranging Our Lives for Spiritual Transformation*. Carol Stream, IL: IVP Books, 2006.

Benner, David. *The Gift of Being Yourself: The Sacred Call to Self-Discovery*. Carol Stream, IL: IVP Books, 2015.

Boers, Arthur. *Living into Focus: Choosing What Matters in an Age of Distractions*. Grand Rapids, MI: Brazos Press, 2012.

Calhoun, Adele Ahlberg. *Spiritual Disciplines Handbook*. Carol Stream, IL: IVP Books, 2015.

Charry, Ellen. *By the Renewing of Your Minds: The Pastoral Function of Christian Doctrine*. New York: Oxford University Press, 1999.

Cofield, James and Richard Plass. *The Relational Soul: Moving from False Self to Deep Connection*. Carol Stream, IL: IVP Books, 2014.

Cuss, Steve. *Managing Leadership Anxiety: Yours and Theirs*. Nashville, TN: Thomas Nelson, 2019.

Earley, Justin Whitmel. *The Common Rule: Habits of Purpose for an Age of Distraction*. Carol Stream, IL: IVP Books, 2019.

Eswine, Zack. *The Imperfect Pastor: Discovering Joy in Our Limitations through a Daily Apprenticeship with Jesus*. Wheaton, IL: Crossway, 2015.

———. *Spurgeon's Sorrows: Realistic Hope for Those Who Suffer from Depression*. Fearn, Ross-shire, UK: Christian Focus, 2015.

Fadling, Alan. *An Unhurried Leader: The Lasting Fruit of Daily Influence*. Carol Stream, IL: IVP Books, 2017.

Hauerwas, Stanley. *The Character of Virtue: Letters to a Godson*. Grand Rapids: Eerdmans, 2021.

Jacobs, Alan. *Breaking Bread with the Dead: A Reader's Guide to a More Tranquil Mind*. New York: Penguin, 2021.

Johnson, Jan, and Dallas Willard. *Renovation of the Heart in Daily Practice: Experiments in Spiritual Transformation*. Colorado Springs, CO: NavPress, 2006.

Kapic, Kelly M. *You're Only Human: How Your Limits Reflect God's Design and Why That's Good News*. Grand Rapids, MI: Brazos Press, 2022.

Kolber, Aundi. *Try Softer: A Fresh Approach to Move Us out of Anxiety, Stress, and Survival Mode—and into a Life of Connection and Joy*. Carol Stream, IL: Tyndale House, 2020.

Moreland, J. P. *Finding Quiet: My Story of Overcoming Anxiety and the Practices that Brought Peace*. Grand Rapids, MI: Zondervan, 2019.

Ortlund, Dane C. *Gentle and Lowly: The Heart of Christ for Sinners and Sufferers*. Wheaton, IL: Crossway, 2020.

Pennington, Jonathan T. *Jesus the Great Philosopher: Rediscovering the Wisdom Needed for the Good Life*. Grand Rapids, MI: Brazos Press, 2020.

Scazzero, Peter. *Emotionally Healthy Discipleship: Moving from Shallow Christianity to Deep Transformation*. Grand Rapids, MI: Zondervan, 2021.

Smith, James Bryan. *The Good and Beautiful God: Falling in Love with the God Jesus Knows.* Carol Stream, IL: IVP Books 2009.

———. *The Good and Beautiful You: Discovering the Person Jesus Created You to Be*. Carol Stream, IL: IVP Books, 2022.

Smith, James K. A. *On the Road with St. Augustine: A Real-World Spirituality for Restless Hearts*. Grand Rapids, MI: Brazos Press, 2019.

———. *You Are What You Love: The Spiritual Power of Habit*. Grand Rapids, MI: Brazos Press, 2016.

Snodgrass, Klyne. *Who God Says You Are: A Christian Understanding of Identity*. Grand Rapids, MI: Eerdmans, 2018.

Song, Felicia Wu. *Restless Devices: Recovering Personhood, Presence, and Place in the Digital Age*. Carol Stream, IL: IVP Academic, 2021.

Strobel, Kyle. *Formed for the Glory of God: Learning from the Spiritual Practices of Jonathan Edwards*. Carol Stream, IL: IVP Books, 2013.

Thompson, Curt. *The Soul of Shame: Retelling the Stories We Believe about Ourselves*. Carol Stream, IL: IVP Books, 2015.

Troxel, A. Craig. *With All Your Heart: Orienting Your Mind, Desires, and Will toward Christ*. Wheaton, IL: Crossway, 2020.

Vroegop, Mark. *Dark Clouds, Deep Mercy: Discovering the Grace of Lament*. Wheaton, IL: Crossway, 2019.

Whitney, Donald. *Praying the Bible*. Wheaton, IL: Crossway, 2015.

Wilder, Jim. *Renovated: God, Dallas Willard, and the Church That Transforms*. Colorado Springs, CO: NavPress, 2020.

Willard, Dallas. *The Spirit of the Disciplines: Understanding How God Changes Lives*. San Francisco, CA: HarperOne, 1999.

Wilkens, Steve, and Mark L. Sanford. *Hidden Worldviews: Eight Cultural Stories that Shape Our Lives*. Carol Stream, IL: IVP Academic, 2009.

Wilkin, Jen. *In His Image: 10 Ways God Calls Us to Reflect His Character*. Wheaton, IL: Crossway, 2018.

———. *Ten Words to Live By: Delighting in and Doing What God Commands*. Wheaton, IL: Crossway, 2021.

———. *Women of the Word: How to Study the Bible with Both Our Hearts and Our Minds*. Wheaton, IL: Crossway, 2019.

Woodson, Elizabeth. *Embrace Your Life: How to Find Joy When the Life You Have Is Not the Life You Hoped For*. Nashville, TN: B&H Publishing Group, 2022.

Revisiting Your Story through Turning Points

THIS TOOL ALLOWS YOU to explore and gain perspective on how you got where you are today in terms of how you think, live, and relate in the world.

A turning point is an event, episode, experience, opportunity, threat, or person that "turns" our life in some way. They can be self-induced—that is, created by our own decisions—or externally driven by an occurrence that happens to or around us. In other words, this is a time when our life came to a point where the direction in at least one life domain (personal, family, vocation, community) was completely altered or "turned" in a different direction (either immediately or as it played out over time). This change can be a drastic turn (examples include marriage, divorce, first child, death of a loved one), or they can be more subtle (a conversation with a person that stuck with you and changed your perspective and trajectory over time, a family vacation, team you made, coach you had, etc.). Ultimately, as you consider each event, the question to ask is: "How did this turn my life?" We can have significant life events that don't end up in an actual change of our thinking, behaviors, or trajectory. By contrast, we can also have seemingly small incidents that do, in fact, turn our lives and set us on a different course.

On the following pages, list possible turning points in your life. As best you can list the age, the turning point, and the specifics of the turn, capturing the internalized messages, changes in paradigm or behaviors. Rate the turning point on a scale of high (10) to low (1). An example might be: Age: 14; Turning Point: Parents divorce; 2; Impact: Home no longer a safe place; I side with Mom; started drinking. Another possibility might be: Age: 17; Turning Point: Coach Turner; 9; Impact: I'm told I'm a leader for the first time; confidence awakened; set me on a course to lead people.[1]

AGE	TURNING POINT	1–10	IMPACT

Acknowledgments

There are many "official and unofficial teachers, through whom Christ has brought me safe thus far," that I owe a debt of gratitude. To my parents, Steve and Julie, and my sister, Cassie—thank you for a life filled with your support and encouragement.

To my wife, Carly, thank you for being my champion. I love you and the life we have together. What a gift.

Dallas, George, Eugene, Jonathan, Klyne, Zack, and Wendell: I am thankful for both the truth you proclaim, and the way you do it. You have marked me as a brother in Christ.

My friends and colleagues who engaged in these ideas with me along the way: Jonathan, Jen, Garrick, Anna, Nathan (both of you), Marissa, Dmitry, Summer, Grant, and Greg—this work is more clear and helpful to me because of you. Thank you.

To my editor, Ashley Gorman, thank you for all your skill and care in seeing this through.

Father, Son, and Holy Spirit—thank you, ever and always. I am grateful to be kept in process under your mighty hand.

Notes

Introduction

1. Klyne R. Snodgrass, *Who God Says You Are: A Christian Understanding of Identity* (Grand Rapids: Eerdmans, 2018), 129.

2. Snodgrass, *Who God Says You Are*, 18.

Section 1

1. M. Basil Pennington, *Thomas Merton: Brother Monk* (New York: Harper & Row, 1987), 19.

Chapter 1

1. This definition of Christian discipleship is one I helped write for The Village Church in the spring of 2022.

2. Alasdair McIntyre, *After Virtue: A Study in Moral Theory* (Notre Dame, IN; University of Notre Dame Press, 2007), 216. Original quote reads: "I can only answer the question, 'What am I to do?' if I can answer the prior question, 'Of what story or stories do I find myself a part?'"

3. Todd Wilson, *The Enneagram Goes to Church: Wisdom for Leadership, Worship, and Congregational Life* (Downers Grove, IL: IVP, 2021), 21.

4. Dallas Willard, The *Spirit of the Disciplines: Understanding How God Changes Lives* (Nashville: HarperCollins, 1999), 6.

5. Felicia Wu Song, *Restless Devices: Recovering Personhood, Presence, and Place in the Digital Age* (Downers Grove, IL: IVP Academic, 2021), 85.

6. Sally Jenkins, "Beneath the Mystery of Tom Brady's Greatness Is a Modest Secret: Self-Discipline," *The Washington Post*, November 12, 2021, https://www.washingtonpost.com/sports/2021/11/12/tom-brady-age-longevity-discipline.

7. Jenkins, "Beneath the Mystery," https://www.washingtonpost.com/sports/2021/11/12/tom-brady-age-longevity-discipline.

8. A. Craig Troxel, *With All Your Heart: Orienting Your Mind, Desires, and Will toward Christ* (Wheaton, IL: Crossway, 2020), 20.

9. John Piper, *Future Grace: The Purifying Power of the Promises of God,* Rev. ed. (Colorado Springs: Multnomah, 2012), 26.

Chapter 2

1. Ellen T. Charry, *By the Renewing of Your Minds: The Pastoral Function of Christian Doctrine* (New York: Oxford University Press, 1999), 3. Also, Dr. Michael Reeves encouraged me in a conversation about this truth that we need to realize God is kind. Good can seem obligatory; God's kindness is from His very heart.

2. Andrew Purves, *Exploring Christology and Atonement: Conversations with John McLeod Campbell, H. R. Mackintosh and T. F. Torrance* (Downers Grove, IL: Academic, 2015), 23. Original quote reads: "If we get God wrong, we get living in the world wrong."

3. Zack Eswine, "The Greatness of an Ordinary Hope," Seven Rivers Presbyterian Church Podcast, July 11, 2017.

4. Jonathan T. Pennington, *The Sermon on the Mount and Human Flourishing: A Theological Commentary* (Grand Rapids: Baker Academic, 2018), 292–93.

5. Michael Reeves, "The Trinity: The Secret to Joyful Christianity," Union School of Theology, accessed August 12, 2022, https://www.uniontheology.org/resources/doctrine/god/the-trinity-the-secret-to-joyful-christianity.

6. Pennington, *The Sermon on the Mount and Human Flourishing*, 293 n. 8.

Chapter 3

1. Dallas Willard, *The Divine Conspiracy: Jesus' Master Class for Life* (Grand Rapids: Zondervan, 2010), 11.

2. Ellen T. Charry, *By the Renewing of Your Minds: The Pastoral Function of Christian Doctrine* (New York: Oxford University Press, 1999), 57.

3. Mark Clavier, *On Consumer Culture, Identity, the Church, and the Rhetorics of Delight* (New York: Bloomsbury Academic, 2018), 11, 47.

4. Clavier, *On Consumer Culture*, 46.

5. Daniel C. Russell, *The Cambridge Companion to Virtue Ethics*, Cambridge Companions to Philosophy (Cambridge: Cambridge University Press, 2013), 35.

6. Russell, *The Cambridge Companion to Virtue Ethics*, 35.

7. Karen Swallow Prior, "Why You Can't Name the Virtues," *Christianity Today*, September 5, 2018, https://www.christianitytoday.com/ct/2018/september-web-only/virtues-why-you-cant-name.html.

8. Dallas Willard, *The Great Omission: Reclaiming Jesus's Essential Teachings on Discipleship* (San Francisco: HarperOne, 2014), 62.

9. Kenneth D. Boa, *Conformed to His Image: Biblical, Practical Approaches to Spiritual Formation*, Rev. ed. (Grand Rapids: Zondervan, 2020), 506. Appendix B in this book is a panoramic view of spiritual formation through Christian history. Boa identifies perennial tensions, some of which I have adapted for discussion here.

10. John Ortberg, *Soul-Keeping: Caring for the Most Important Part of You* (Grand Rapids: Zondervan, 2014), 19. Dallas Willard is well known for saying: "The most important thing in your life is not what you do; it's who you become. That's what you will take into eternity. You are an unceasing spiritual being with an eternal destiny in God's universe."

11. Klyne R. Snodgrass, *Who God Says You Are: A Christian Understanding of Identity* (Grand Rapids: Eerdmans, 2018), 7.

12. Blaise Pascal, *Pensées*, no. 547 in Snodgrass, *Who God Says You Are*, 7.

13. John Calvin, *Institutes of the Christian Religion*, 2.16.3 in Andrew Purves, *Exploring Christology and Atonement: Conversations with John McLeod Campbell, H. R. Mackintosh and T. F. Torrance* (Downers Grove, IL: Academic, 2015).

Interlude

1. Jonathan Edwards, "Christ Is to the Heart like a River to a Tree Planted by It," in *Sermons and Discourses, 1743–1758*, ed. Wilson H. Kimnach and Harry S. Stout, Vol. 25, *The Works of Jonathan Edwards* (New Haven, London: Yale University Press, 2006), 600–604.

Chapter 4

1. This concept of abiding in technology can be found in Felicia Wu Song, *Restless Devices: Recovering Personhood, Presence, and Place in the Digital Age* (Downers Grove: IVP Academic, 2021), 22.

2. See Tristan Harris, "Your Undivided Attention," a podcast, https://www.humanetech.com/podcast, and "The Social Dilemma," a documentary, https://www.humanetech.com/the-social-dilemma, Center for Humane Technology, accessed August 12, 2022.

3. Sherry Turkle, *Reclaiming Conversation: The Power of Talk in a Digital Age* (New York: Penguin Books, 2016), 126.

4. Rachael Kent, "Self-Tracking Health over Time: From the Use of Instagram to Perform Optimal Health to the Protective Shield of the Digital Detox, *Social Media + Society* (July–September 2020): 1–14.

5. Albert Borgmann, *Technology and the Character of Contemporary Life: A Philosophical Inquiry* (Chicago: University of Chicago Press, 1987), 41.

6. Borgmann, *Technology and the Character of Contemporary Life*, 48.

7. Mark Clavier, *On Consumer Culture, Identity, the Church, and the Rhetoric of Delight* (New York: Bloomsbury Academic, 2018), 85.

Chapter 5

1. A. Craig Troxel, *With All Your Heart: Orienting Your Mind, Desires, and Will toward Christ* (Wheaton, IL: Crossway, 2020), 18–20.

2. John Webster, *God without Measure: Working Papers in Christian Theology: Vol. 1, God and the Works of God* (London: T&T Clark, 2018), 183.

3. John Calvin, *Institutes of the Christian Religion,* Vol 1, ed. John T. McNeill, trans. Ford Lewis Battles (Philadelphia: Westminster Press, 1960), 39.

4. Ellen T. Charry, *By the Renewing of Your Minds: The Pastoral Function of Christian Doctrine* (New York: Oxford University Press, 1999), 225.

5. This side-by-side, face-to-face concept is adapted from Rob Murray, Jack Nicholson, Jerome Daley, *The Human Operating System: Recovering the Heart and Soul of Your Leadership* (n.p.: Transformed Leader, 2021).

6. Jen Wilkin, *Women of the Word: How to Study the Bible with Both Our Hearts and Our Minds* (Wheaton, IL: Crossway, 2019), 24.

7. Dallas Willard, *The Divine Conspiracy: Jesus' Master Class for Life* (Grand Rapids: Zondervan, 2010), 11.

8. Jan Johnson, *Meeting God in Scripture: A Hands-On Guide to Lection Divina* (Downers Grove, IL: IVP Books, 2016), 13.

9. C. S. Lewis, "Preface" from Athanasius, *On the Incarnation* (Yonkers, NY: St. Vladimir's Seminary Press, 2021), 1–2.

10. John Piper, Tweet, November 25, 2013, https://twitter.com/johnpiper/status/404973861034553344?lang=en.

11. Willard, *The Divine Conspiracy*, 11.

12. Wilkin, *Women of the Word*, 33.

13. Wilkin, *Women of the Word*, 33.

14. Adapted from the "My Story" video on thevillagechurch.net, https://vimeo.com/408073132/ceeeda1c0b.

Chapter 6

1. John Ortberg, *Soul-Keeping: Caring for the Most Important Part of You* (Grand Rapids: Zondervan, 2014), 20.

2. Klyne R. Snodgrass, *Stories with Intent: A Comprehensive Guide to the Parables of Jesus* (Grand Rapids: Eerdmans, 2018), 145–46.

3. Snodgrass, *Stories with Intent*, 146.

4. Zack Eswine, *The Imperfect Pastor: Discovering Joy in Our Limitations through a Daily Apprenticeship with Jesus* (Wheaton, IL: Crossway, 2015), 89.

5. Alan Fadling, *An Unhurried Life: Following Jesus' Rhythms of Work and Rest* (Downers Grove, IL: IVP, 2020), 15.

Dimension Two

1. Wendell Berry, *The Peace of Wild Things* (New York: Penguin, 2018), 105.

Chapter 7

1. Aundi Kolber, *Try Softer: A Fresh Approach to Move Us out of Anxiety, Stress, and Survival Mode—and into a Life of Connection and Joy* (Carol Stream, IL: Tyndale House, 2020), 170.

2. The Feelings Wheel, Calm, accessed August 13, 2022, https://blog.calm.com/blog/the-feelings-wheel.

3. Zack Eswine, *The Imperfect Pastor: Discovering Joy in Our Limitations through a Daily Apprenticship with Jesus* (Wheaton, IL: Crossway, 2015), 172–84. My description here is adapted from a blog I wrote for The Village Church: "The Frustration of Slowing Down," May 24, 2016, https://www.tvcresources.net/resource-library/articles/the-frustration-of-slowing-down.

4. Tom Paterson, *Living the Life You Were Meant to Live* (Nashville: Thomas Nelson, 1998), 90–137.

5. Klyne R. Snodgrass, *Who God Says You Are: A Christian Understanding of Identity* (Grand Rapids: Eerdmans, 2018), 75.

6. Description of Turning Points adapted from TVC Leadership Turning Point description, https://thevillagechurch.net/content/external site/leadership/turning_points.pdf (used with permission).

7. Curt Thompson, *The Soul of Shame: Retelling the Stories We Believe about Ourselves* (Carol Stream, IL: IVP, 2015), 138.

8. Sam Allberry, "I Trust Them with My Sins: Four Ways to Welcome Confession," guest contributor, Desiring God, February 28, 2022, https://www.desiringgod.org/articles/i-trust-them-with-my-sins.

9. Thompson, *The Soul of Shame*, 136.

Chapter 8

1. Eugene Peterson, *Answering God: The Psalms as Tool for Prayer* (San Francisco: HarperOne, 1991), 5.

2. John Calvin and James Anderson, *Commentary on the Book of Psalms,* Vol. 1 (Bellingham, WA: Logos Bible Software, 2010), xxxvi–xxxvii.

3. Frederick Buechner, *A Room Called Remember: Uncollected Pieces* (San Francisco: HarperOne, 1992), 11.

4. Donald S. Whitney, *Praying the Bible* (Wheaton: Crossway, 2015), 51.

5. Whitney, *Praying the Bible*, 52.

6. See Mark Vroegop, *Dark Clouds, Deep Mercy: Discovering the Grace of Lament* (Wheaton, IL: Crossway, 2019), 37, for the exact quotation (Kindle). And though I did not word it as he did, let the reader note that the concept of lament being a space held between pain and promise also comes from Vroegop's book.

7. Vroegop, *Dark Clouds, Deep Mercy*, 37.

8. Ivan Mesa, "Sandra McCracken on Life, Loss, and Longing in the Psalms," The Gospel Coalition, May 21, 2015, https://www.thegospel coalition.org/article/sandra-mccracken-psalms.

9. K. J. Ramsey, "Scripture and Neuroscience Agree: It Helps to Lament in Community," *Christianity Today*, November 15, 2019, https:// www.christianitytoday.com/ct/2019/november-web-only/neuroscience -and-scripture-agree-it-helps-to-lament-in-comm.html.

10. Mesa, "Sandra McCracken on Life, Loss, and Longing in the Psalms."

11. Brene Brown, "The Price of Invulnerability," TEDxKC, October 12, 2012, https://www.youtube.com/watch?v=_UoMXF73j0c.

12. Brown, "The Price of Invulnerability."

13. Klyne R. Snodgrass, *Stories with Intent: A Comprehensive Guide to the Parables of Jesus* (Grand Rapids, Eerdmans, 2018).

14. Snodgrass, *Stories with Intent*, 121.

15. Snodgrass, *Stories with Intent*, 121.

Dimension Three

1. Charles Péguy, *Basic Verities: Poetry and Prose* (New York: Pantheon Books, 1943), 209–11.

Chapter 9

1. See Matthew 20:32; Mark 10:36, 51; and Luke 18:41.

2. Michael W. Austin and R. Douglas Geivett, *Being Good: Christian Virtues for Everyday Life* (Grand Rapids: Eerdmans, 2011), 66–69.

3. H. D. M. Spence-Jones, ed., *Psalms,* Vol. 3, *The Pulpit Commentary* (New York: Funk & Wagnalls, 1909), 256.

4. David Powlison, "Peace, Be Still: Learning Psalm 131 by Heart," *Journal of Biblical Counseling*, vol. 18, no. 3, Spring 2000, 3. This article has shaped my understanding and engagement with the text. I am grateful for the enduring work Powlison spent applying the Scriptures to the human experience. It is well worth reading it for yourself: https://www.ccef.org/wp-content/uploads/2016/09/Peace-be-still-Learning-Psalm-131-by-Heart.pdf.

5. Mark Clavier, *On Consumer Culture, Identity, the Church, and the Rhetorics of Delight* (New York: Bloomsbury Academic, 2018), 15.

6. David F. Wells, *Losing Our Virtue: Why the Church Must Recover Its Moral Vision* (Grand Rapids: Eerdmans, 1999), 12–13.

7. I originally used this language in a sermon preached at my church: Mason King, "Entering God's Rest," The Village Church,

September 9, 2019, https://www.thevillagechurch.net/resources/sermons/entering-gods-rest.

8. Arthur Boers, *Living into Focus: Choosing What Matters in an Age of Distractions* (Grand Rapids: Brazos, 2012), 185.

9. Boers, *Living into Focus,* 186.

Chapter 10

1. William Shakespeare, Harold Bloom, and Burton Raffel, *Hamlet* (New Haven: Yale University Press, 2003), 94.

2. "You've Got to Find What You Love," Jobs Says," Stanford University News, June 14, 2005, https://news.stanford.edu/2005/06/14/jobs-061505.

3. Jonathan Edwards, *Letters and Personal Writings*, ed. George S. Claghorn and Harry S. Stout, Vol. 16, *The Works of Jonathan Edwards* (New Haven: Yale University Press, 1998), 753.

4. M. Basil Pennington, *Thomas Merton: Brother Monk* (New York: Harper & Row, 1987), 19.

Conclusion

1. C. S. Lewis, *Letters to Malcolm: Chiefly on Prayer* (San Francisco: HarperOne, 2017).

2. Jonathan Edwards, "Christ Is to the Heart like a River to a Tree Planted by It," in *Sermons and Discourses, 1743–1758*, ed. Wilson H. Kimnach and Harry S. Stout, Vol. 25, *The Works of Jonathan Edwards* (New Haven, London: Yale University Press, 2006), 600–604.

Revisiting Your Story through Turning Points

1. This adaptation is used with permission from The Paterson Center (creator of the original tool) as seen at https://patersoncenter.com/wp-content/uploads/2021/10/Paterson-LifePlan-Prework.pdf and from The Village Church, who uses its own adapted version of the tool as seen at https://thevillagechurch.net/content/externalsite/leadership/turning_points.pdf.